# ASPIRATION VS. OPPORTUNITY: "CAREERS" IN THE INNER CITY

Policy Papers in Human Resources
and Industrial Relations, 20

# ASPIRATION VS. OPPORTUNITY: "CAREERS" IN THE INNER CITY

# Paul Bullock

*with the research assistance of*

**JACOBO RODRIGUEZ**

*and the survey and technical assistance of*

| | |
|---|---|
| Gilbert Armendariz | Victor Padilla |
| Teresa Caballero | Eduardo Perez |
| Ruben Ceballos | Jimmy Perez |
| Richard Ceja | Gary Pope |
| James Currie | Yvonne Rippon |
| Miguel Gastinell | Jesse Simmons, Jr. |
| Stephanie Green | William Smith |
| Randy Jackson | Paul A. Williams |
| Javier Muniz | Wenfred Womack |

ANN ARBOR, MICHIGAN
INSTITUTE OF LABOR AND INDUSTRIAL RELATIONS
THE UNIVERSITY OF MICHIGAN—WAYNE STATE UNIVERSITY
1973

Library of Congress Catalog Number: 73-620101
International Standard Book Number
ISBN:  cloth  87736-122-3
       paper  87736-123-1

Manufactured in the United States of America

The material in this book was prepared under Institutional Grant No. 31-05-70-07-B from the Manpower Administration, United States Department of Labor, under the authority of Title I of the Manpower Development and Training Act of 1962, as amended. Researchers undertaking such projects under Government sponsorship are encouraged to express freely their professional judgment. Therefore, points of view or opinions stated in this document do not necessarily represent the official position or policy of the Department of Labor. Moreover, the researcher is solely responsible for the factual accuracy of all material developed in this book.

# ACKNOWLEDGMENTS

In the arduous and sometimes frustrating process of conducting this study of youth employment patterns and career aspirations in the Black and Chicano communities of Los Angeles, I have had invaluable help and cooperation from many persons. Particularly valuable was the assistance given me by several of the young men and women who live in these communities and who were mainly responsible for administering and processing the interviews, and I have listed their names on the title page as major contributors to whatever merit this study may have.

Much of the research and data collection for this study has been ably performed by Jacobo Rodriguez, Community Services Representative on the staff of the Institute of Industrial Relations. The steering committee of the IIR Manpower Research Center, one of several institutional centers funded by the U.S. Department of Labor, authorized the original grant which supported the study. I am particularly grateful to the following Institute members who typed and helped duplicate the manuscript: Shirley Matthews, Janis Okida, Lily Robillard, Patricia Tamayo, and Monika Weber. I am equally indebted to the staff of the UCLA Survey Research Center for efficient assistance in the final processing of the survey data.

This book is a product of the research program of the Institute of Industrial Relations. Needless to say, I alone am responsible for the interpretations, conclusions, and recommendations contained herein.

PAUL BULLOCK
Research Economist
Institute of Industrial Relations
UCLA

*September, 1972*

# CONTENTS

Acknowledgments    v

1.  Introduction    3

2.  The Youth Labor Market: An Overview    23

3.  Counseling and the School Experience    43

4.  Entering the Labor Market    57

5.  Labor Market Information and Perceptions    71

6.  Choosing a Career    87

7.  The Subeconomy    99

8.  The Subeconomy in American History    127

9.  Special Obstacles to Youth Employment    149

10.  Toward the Future    163

# ASPIRATION VS. OPPORTUNITY: "CAREERS" IN THE INNER CITY

# 1

## INTRODUCTION

This is a study of the process by which young men in low income
Black and Chicano ghettos enter the labor market. Of the identifia-
ble groups whose employment experience is reported and evalu-
ated in official censuses and surveys, none has suffered a higher
and more persistent rate of unemployment than has the minority
youth labor force. Indeed, massive unemployment and underemployment have prevailed in urban ghettos even during periods of
significant economic growth and general prosperity. In 1969, when
the overall male unemployment rate was only 2.8 percent, the
officially reported rate for Negro male teenagers was 21.3 percent
and the rate for those in the age 20-24 bracket was 8.4 percent. In
1970, a year of economic recession, the corresponding rates for
Negro male teenagers and young adults were 24.8 percent and
12.6 percent respectively at a time when the overall male unemployment rate had risen to 4.4 percent. Though the rate of youth
unemployment is sensitive to changes in the rate of economic
growth, since 1954 (after the end of the Korean war in 1953) the
annual unemployment rate for Black male teenagers has never

fallen below 13.4 percent, and over the decade of the 1960s the rate never dropped below 21.3 percent.[1] As of March 1971 the reported unemployment rate for nonwhite men in the age 16-24 bracket was 20.1 percent (compared with a rate of 12.7 percent for white men in that same category, "white" being defined so as to include almost all persons of Latin origin such as Puerto Ricans and Mexican Americans). [2]

Consistent time series for the Chicano youth population are either unavailable or highly inadequate relative to the quantity and quality of data on young Blacks in the labor market. A recent study, however, gives an unemployment rate of 14.3 percent for Chicano men in the age 16-24 bracket, as of March 1971.[3] This compares with a reported rate of approximately 10 percent for that same category in November 1969.[4]

Clearly there is a chronic problem of unemployment and underemployment among minority youngsters which persists despite cyclical movements, or even secular growth, in aggregate indices such as Gross National Product and total employment. Strong economic growth and full employment policies are a necessary but *not* a sufficient condition for measurable improvement in the economic status of minority young men residing in central city ghettos. Now can it be assumed that the income earned by a Black youngster in a low income area is merely a supplement to the earnings of a fully employed adult head of household. Most of the young people in a community like Watts live in households headed by a mother on welfare or in intermittent, low-paid employment, or an adult man who is unemployed or underemployed, or, often times, headed by themselves. Thus the lack of employment has disastrous consequences both for the individual and for the household.

Nor does frequent job changing and intermittency of employment generally have the beneficial side effects which may be advantageous to young people in higher-income areas. The jobs available to a ghetto or barrio resident, particularly to a teenager or young adult, are not of a diverse nature which might provide an exposure to varying occupational experiences and a useful introduction to the labor market.

The basic problem, however, is even more complex than the official statistics might suggest. A high proportion of men are not enumerated in the censuses and surveys on which the published reports have been based—a fact which in recent years has been acknowledged by the census takers themselves. The undercount appears to be greatest among men in the age 20-50 bracket who are nonwhite and concentrated in low-income, low-skilled categories. "The 1960 census enumerated 98 percent of white persons but only 90 percent of persons of other races, according to Census Bureau estimates. The total number of unenumerated persons has been estimated to be 5.7 million, of whom 38 percent were members of races other than white. Thus while the number of uncounted white persons is greater than the number of uncounted persons of other races, the proportion of white persons missed is considerably smaller than the proportion of persons of other races."[5]

Special studies of unenumerated persons in New Haven, Connecticut, central Harlem in New York City, and Trenton, New Jersey, have produced some tentative conclusions about the characteristics of nonwhite men missed in the official census. Uncounted men are less likely to be married, and are more likely to move frequently, than are those who are enumerated. In the studies mentioned, there is little evidence to suggest that inclusion of the previously unenumerated men would significantly affect the total unemployment rate, although the sample is regarded as too small to justify conclusive findings.[6] Further, it would appear that any study of this nature would necessarily experience many of the obstacles which earlier enumerations have encountered: principally, a reluctance of many unenumerated persons to give employment and other socioeconomic information to unfamiliar interviewers. An additional factor, to be explored at greater length later, is the somewhat obscure meaning of terms like "employment" and "unemployment" in a low-income ghetto where attachment to the labor force, *as formally defined*, is subject to unique variations and influences. Some preliminary estimates of undercount in the 1970 census suggest that significant percentages of persons were also missed then (perhaps as many as in 1960), thus indicating that the problem of the "invisible man" is a continuing one. We know, in addition, that large numbers of "discouraged workers" simply drop out of the labor market.

A recent report of the Advisory Committee on Problems of Census Enumeration further emphasizes the importance of gaps in the census data. "The crux of recent concern about census underenumeration is less the simple 3 percent shortfall in *national census totals* than much larger deficiencies in the counts of *specific population subgroups*, most notably young black men."[7] Noting that approximately 15 percent of all nonwhite men between the ages of 20 and 40 are estimated not to have been counted in the census, it adds that the Current Population Survey (CPS) figures also suffer from the problem of underenumeration and that one out of four young adult nonwhite males is thought to be unrepresented in the CPS samples.[8] The committee's report finds that many of the concepts and assumptions upon which the census is based are inappropriate to the life styles of various groups within American society, and that "in urban slums and tenements, there are people whose existence and whereabouts will not be acknowledged by anyone."[9] In specific economic terms, it notes that "definitions of work and income are, for some people, extremely loose. Their sources of income are varied and often cannot be broken down into wages, salaries, commissions, and the like. Among ghetto residents, for example, information about income is not readily volunteered to anyone, and the census is, of course, not apt to be informed of income derived from illegal businesses or from welfare checks for which the recipient-respondent is legally ineligible."[10]

The official discovery of "missing men" in the censuses underscores a point which others have made unofficially: that minorities in America have traditionally been undercounted, and that large numbers exist in a shadowy no man's land which is neither fully in nor fully out of the labor market. Close observers of economic conditions in inner city ghettos have long been puzzled by the apparent gap in magnitude between the amount of unemployment or underemployment or poverty observed and the amount reported in official censuses and studies.[11]

On the other hand, common sense alone has suggested that persons who are unemployed and not receiving "welfare" or unemployment compensation or any other form of special assistance *must* have access to some means of livelihood in order to survive.[12] Though malnutrition and unbalanced diets are serious national problems, most of those in the poverty category somehow manage to avoid starvation and eke out a minimal living. Thus it is reasonable to conclude that some form of income-producing activity prevails which has not been fully chronicled.

After decades of almost total neglect, the possible economic importance of such activity is finally receiving some public attention. Sociological studies such as Elliot Liebow's *Tally's Corner* have triggered awareness of and interest in the "street society," and the 1971 *Manpower Report of the President* (in the section prepared by the Department of Labor) devotes five paragraphs to a discussion of "illegal activities," citing a recent Harlem study which concludes that about two of every five adult inhabitants had some illegal income in 1966 and that one in five seemed to exist *entirely* on money gained from illegal sources.[13]

The demonstrated inadequacy of more formal research processes emphasizes the need to supplement traditional techniques of social inquiry with informal (and necessarily more subjective) tools of fact-gathering and analysis. Although structured survey interviewing has been used in the present study, it has been supplemented by free-wheeling taped interviews with small groups of young men and women who live in the east Los Angeles and Watts areas. Thus the "research" in this study represents a partnership between the author and members of the group which, in a sense, is being studied. In most cases I have been acquainted with the interviewees for several years, though this is considerably more true of the south Los Angeles interviews than it is of the east Los Angeles. Everyone interviewed was assured that his or her anonymity would be protected. In all cases the responses appeared to be frank and open.

The interviews focus upon two subject categories whose relationship will subsequently be clear to the reader: (1) the quantity and quality of labor market information received by young people and its effect upon career aspirations and job search; and (2) the economic impact of the illegal "soft drug" (marijuana and pills) industry in the community. Information on the first subject has been collected both from the formal surveys and from interviews; information on the second has been gathered entirely from interviews or from published materials such as financial statements, Congressional hearings and government reports, and other sources of data on the drug traffic in the United States.

A word about the geography of Greater Los Angeles may help to put our survey areas into perspective. A sprawling decentralized megalopolis, Los Angeles County exhibits both the benefits and defects of size. Diversity is, perhaps, its most attractive characteristic: mountains, deserts, and beaches are within a one or two hour drive from almost any community in the county, and the City of Los Angeles itself is so vast that many areas designated elsewhere as suburbs are actually a part of the city. For instance, the mammoth San Fernando Valley is (with some exceptions like the city of San Fernando) within the Los Angeles city limits, but is predominantly suburban and contains so many residents that it would be a major city even if it were incorporated separately.

With size and space, of course, go complex problems. The public transportation system is abominable: hundreds of thousands of cars clog the freeways and pollute the air; open space is diminishing and, for the first time, skyscrapers and boxlike, uninspiring office buildings begin to dominate the skyline. Even the weather—that seemingly reliable lure for millions of newcomers over the decades—plays tricks. "Santa Ana" winds and atmospheric conditions cause alternating spells of heat and cold, and massive, unstoppable fires rage through the hills and valleys almost yearly. Yet the population continues upward, though perhaps at a slower pace, and more and more "natives" move toward the fringes of the county or even into adjoining counties, far from the rapidly declining downtown area.

As in so many other cities, the central city has been reserved for the minorities. The major Chicano and Black ghettos are linked closely to the core of Los Angeles, with a huge Mexican American barrio extending eastward from downtown and an equally impressive Negro ghetto covering about fifty or sixty square miles to the south and to the west. The Chicanos constitute by far the largest minority in the county (it is said that only Mexico City and Guadalajara in Mexico exceed Greater Los Angeles in population of Mexican origin), outnumbering the Blacks by about 500,000.[14] The Chicano population, however, is less concentrated than the Black: about three-quarters of the Blacks in the county live in the sprawling central ghetto, while less than half of the Mexican Americans are located in Greater East Los Angeles. The ghetto, of course, is not economically or socially homogeneous: the southeastern section of the segregated Black population tends to be poor, but the western areas contain many who have pleasant homes and reasonably good incomes.

Housing segregation is burdensome for Blacks and Chicanos in many respects. Centers of employment tend to move farther from the central city, but transportation is inefficient or costly and the minorities have fewer options on residential location. The quality of education and public services declines as the Anglos leave, transferring their wealth and their power to the suburbs. Yet, ironically, their relatively greater residential concentration within the city and county gives the Blacks at least some political advantage over the Chicanos, since the Black population can centralize and coordinate its voting strength more effectively. As a result, there are three Blacks, and no Chicanos, on the Los Angeles City Council.

In the Black community of Los Angeles, our survey focused principally on the Watts area—geographically a small part of the central ghetto—nestled in the southeastern section of the city and traditionally characterized by poverty and unemployment. The vast majority of teenagers surveyed live either in Watts, as narrowly defined, or in neighborhoods within two or three miles from Watts. Even among the young adults interviewed, probably most of them had at least formerly lived in Watts and a great many continue to live there or have parents, other relatives, or close friends located there, even though they themselves may currently live on or near a college campus or at some other location outside of Watts. Thus our survey area in the Black community was reasonably compact. In the following text, the terms "Watts area" and "south Los Angeles" are used interchangeably, denoting a contiguous section roughly coterminous with the "Concentrated Employment Program (CEP)" area used in the Urban Employment Survey in 1968-1969.

The area surveyed in the Chicano community was less concentrated geographically and, apparently, was somewhat more heterogeneous economically and socially. It covered much of what is labeled as "east Los Angeles", an area encompassing a part of the City of Los Angeles and a large unincorporated community within the jurisdiction of County government. The interviewing, however, also took place in Chicano neighborhoods in the nearby towns of Montebello and Monterey Park, as well as in another predominantly Latin neighborhood of Los Angeles known as Pico-Union. Some of the possible effects of such characteristics of the Chicano survey area are suggested later, but apparently our sampling yielded results which conform reasonably well (wherever comparisons can be made) to the findings of the Census Employment

Survey conducted by the Census Bureau in certain Chicano and Black areas of Los Angeles, not identical with ours, in late 1970.

The survey sample was selected on a "judgmental" rather than a "random" basis. There were many reasons for this, but perhaps the decisive one was that we wanted to assure maximum rapport between interviewer and interviewee and maximum accuracy and frankness in the responses to questions which inevitably explored matters of great sensitivity. A "random" sample is of little value if the answers obtained are incorrect or seriously incomplete; on the other hand, a "judgment" sample cannot produce valid generalizations (even assuming that the responses are honest) if the sampling is unduly biased or unrepresentative of the larger group. We decided to identify young men and women who live in the communities to be surveyed, and ask them to interview friends, acquaintances, schoolmates, fellow gang members, and others in the general area falling within the appropriate age range. Despite the increasingly formidable barriers to "surveys" in low-income neighborhoods, and with the qualifications indicated in other parts of this study, the process has seemed to function with reasonable effectiveness and, indeed, somewhat better than first anticipated.

There is, of course, a general resistance to surveys, stemming from a suspicion of the interviewers' motives, an impatience with the time consumed and the boredom required, and a fervent belief that it is all an exercise in academic "make work" which, at best, only proves what everyone already knows. There is some merit in each of these complaints, but we attempted, with at least partial success, to overcome such resistance by employing as interviewers young men and women from Watts and east Los Angeles who are in the same age group as those interviewed. As a consequence, we obtained 304 usable interviews in Watts and 268 in east Los Angeles, with the bulk of the Watts interviews conducted in the spring and early summer of 1971, and the bulk of the east Los Angeles interviews in mid-summer.

In studies of this nature, complex problems arise in connection with the usual definitions of labor market status. However clear or unclear the meanings of "employment," "unemployment," and "labor force" may be in other areas, they are decidedly obscure and uncertain in communities such as Watts and east Los Angeles. For instance, we sought initially to use the normal definition of "unemployed," which reflects an assumption that the interviewee is neither in school full time nor in a job *and* has been actively seeking work over a defined period, such as the previous week (or, in the case of the Department of Labor and Census Bureau definition, the previous four weeks). In test interviews, however, we discovered that this question posed knotty problems for the interviewer, since the respondent may not have been then "looking for work" even though he met the other criteria for being unemployed. Furthermore, he may have been "self-employed" at least in the degree that he had been "hustling" for income on the street. In such a case, he probably should be classified as "employed," in strictly economic terms, and the implications of this are explored more fully in Chapter VII. For our purposes, however, we had to decide whether he was "unemployed" or "out of the labor force," that is, a discouraged worker, and we opted for the classification of "unemployed" unless he provided clear evidence to the contrary. These are, obviously, fine lines of distinction which call into question the usefulness of certain of the traditional labor-market definitions used.

Another possible problem is the tendency of some respondents to classify themselves as "employed" when, in fact, they are not. While employment as such may not confer any status upon the interviewee within his immediate peer group, it may be perceived as being more acceptable in the eyes of the usual interviewer. The fact that we used local residents as interviewers may have eased this problem, though conceivably it introduced other difficulties. Perhaps of greater importance is the fact that, for some young people in the ghetto or barrio, it is to their interest to be officially classified as "employed," or at least as persons who are actively seeking employment. Probation and parole officers, for example, often will view the youngster more favorably if he reports himself as "employed," and some young men may occasionally make an arrangement with a friend or a kindly disposed businessman to report them as "employees" if a probation officer or other official should inquire.

These considerations may tend somewhat to offset one another, and it is impossible to determine how the actual "unemployment" rate ultimately is affected by them. A related problem is the probability that some respondents are quite honestly uncertain or confused about their employment status at the time of interview, and may be inclined to classify themselves as "employed" even though they are on layoff or otherwise receiving no current income from a job. The status of the Watts survey interviewers themselves could be a case in point, since they remain technically on the UCLA payroll even as these words are written and yet receive no income because no hours worked are being reported.

Whatever relative weights are given to these various considerations and difficulties, it is clear and incontrovertible that unemployment in Watts and east Los Angeles is of crisis proportions. When those who were in school or otherwise out of the labor force are deducted from the statistics, the total unemployment rates for all men ages 16 to 24 in our sample are approximately 46 percent in Watts and 30 percent in east Los Angeles. For the teenage (ages 16 to 19) group alone, the respective rates are 62 percent and 34 percent. Even if it can be concluded that some part of this differential in rates between the two areas is due to a sampling bias (the sample from east Los Angeles is substantially better off economically than the Watts sample, according to survey estimates of family incomes, but on the other hand, many Chicanos were out of school and in the summer labor market at the time of interview), all rates are shockingly high and the general pattern is consistent with the findings of the Urban Employment Survey in similar areas in 1968-1969.[15]

Figures on labor force participation are especially dubious and subject to much interpretation in inner city areas, if not generally, but again participation tends to be higher among young men in the predominantly Chicano area than in the Black area surveyed, and young Chicanos are relatively more successful in finding work, although in both cases the jobs are concentrated *below* the skilled or professional levels. Overall figures on labor force participation are influenced by the different periods over which the surveys were conducted. Nevertheless, tabulations by age and school status continue to show that young Chicanos participate in the labor force in higher relative numbers than do young Blacks.

At the time of the surveys, the vast majority of Chicano teenagers (65 percent) were in the labor market, due to the fact that many of them were seeking summertime jobs, while only 38 percent of the Black teenagers could be counted as being in the labor force because many were still in school at survey time. A more representative pattern emerges from the sampling of young adults (ages 20 to 24) in the two areas: in this group, approximately 74 percent of Chicanos and 68 percent of Blacks participated in the labor force at survey time.

Proportionately more Black teenagers (70 percent) attend school than do Chicano teenagers (62 percent), which probably accounts for a part of the difference in labor force participation in that age group.[16] Among young adults in our sampling, however, the percentages of school attendance were virtually identical: approximately 29 percent in each area surveyed. Among those reported as not attending any school, dropout rates reflect a mixed pattern. An astounding 54 percent of the south Los Angeles teenagers had dropped out of school without getting a diploma, while the corresponding figure for east Los Angeles teenagers was 33 percent— still high but much lower than the rate in Watts. The relationship is reversed for young adults surveyed: 22 percent in south Los Angeles and 32 percent in east Los Angeles.[17]

Most of the young men in south Los Angeles attend or have attended either David Starr Jordan or Alain Locke High School, both located in the general Watts area. Locke is a relatively new school and a dropout ("attrition") figure is available only for its 1970 graduating class, indicating that about 23 percent of the 1967 entry classes (adjusted) had failed to graduate. Jordan probably enrolls a bigger percentage of the student population of Watts as narrowly defined, and is an older school in the system, located near junkyards, a noisy manufacturing plant, and a massive public housing project. Its dropout figures in recent years are quite consistent with our own findings for teenagers in Watts, particularly when it is considered that males invariably drop out more frequently than females and that some young men will drop out before entering senior high school. Our dropout percentages for east Los Angeles also are consistent with available figures for the public schools in that area, but many youngsters in that sample have attended or do attend private schools or schools outside the Los Angeles district, with some effects which are suggested later.

It is possible, of course, that figures on educational attainment and other variables, in both east and south Los Angeles, could have been affected by in-migration and the accompanying fact that education had been obtained in areas outside of Los Angeles County. Our statistics on length of residence in the county, however, refute this possibility. Of the total sample, approximately 61 percent in south Los Angeles and 80 percent in east Los Angeles reported that they had lived in Los Angeles County *all their lives.* Only about 5 percent of the Blacks and 1 percent of the Chicanos had been in the county less than one year at the time of survey. The evidence is overwhelming, therefore, that almost all of the persons surveyed had attended, or are attending, senior high schools in Los Angeles County. It also suggests, quite clearly, that the many economic and social problems affecting both groups are not connected with recent in-migration.

Figures on marital status and "head of household" show that this is overwhelmingly an unmarried group, in both areas, and that about 60 percent of Watts teenagers live in households headed by someone other than their fathers. By contrast, two thirds of east Los Angeles teenagers live in households headed by their fathers. Perhaps a more unexpected result is that almost a fifth of all east Los Angeles interviewees live in households headed by their mothers, and another 6 percent live in households headed by a sibling, other relative, or someone else beside a parent or them- selves. Among Chicano teenagers alone, the percentage living in households headed by a mother is approximately 22 percent, and approximately another 5 percent live in households headed by someone other than a parent or themselves. This degree of family disorganization—affecting about one quarter of all respondents in a predominantly Chicano area—was not anticipated.

The figures on marital status are skewed somewhat by the fact that the proportion of young teenagers is much higher in the east Los Angeles sample than in the south Los Angeles. Despite this, probably not more than a third of the Chicano young adults in our sample are married, and less than a fifth of the Black adults report that they are married (with wife present in household.) Obviously, our survey tells much more about the problems and prospects of single men in the two areas than about those of married men.

Survey results also suggest that households tend to be large in both areas surveyed, markedly more so for teenagers than for young adults, as would be expected. The average size of household appears to be somewhat larger in east than in south Los Angeles, but this can be accounted for by the fact that there are propor- tionately more young teenagers in the east Los Angeles sample.

Family income figures, highly unreliable at best, indicate that the average household income is considerably higher in the east Los Angeles sample than in the south Los Angeles, but many qualifications must be added here. Of those responding to the question in each area, about 35 percent of Watts area respondents are listed as being in households receiving less than $4000 a year, compared to about 15 percent of the east Los Angeles group. On the other hand, only about 17 percent of the Watts respondents are in households receiving more than $6000 a year in income, contrasted with almost 48 percent of the east Los Angeles sample responding to that question. Among teenagers, about 84 percent of Watts youngsters were reported as being in households receiving $6000 a year *or less*, compared to only 42 percent of the east Los Angeles group.[18]

What these considerations may indicate, in general, is that our sample probably contains a somewhat higher percentage of middle-income households than is true for east Los Angeles, narrowly defined, but that (given the probable impact of nonresponses and other factors) the difference between the east and south Los Angeles samples is not as wide as the family income figures alone would suggest. Clearly, the teenage group in Watts can be regarded as "hard core" (a term which is intended merely to reflect extreme economic deprivation). The corresponding group in east Los Angeles is somewhat less so, but this fact, in a sense, gives even more dramatic impact to the severe economic and educational problems spotlighted in our study.

Perhaps we should add a final word of warning about the usefulness of family income figures as they may apply to areas such as Watts and east Los Angeles. As I have mentioned earlier and will explore deeply in Chapter VII, reported income often will not include total income from all sources, especially those which may be illegal or illicit. On the other hand, some respondents probably tend, for reasons of preceived status or related factors, to exaggerate the amount of income actually received. Under any circumstances, questions about income and personal finance are perhaps more resented and suspected than any others contained in the typical household survey. Even where there is no intent on the part of the interviewee to conceal any information, there is the omnipresent problem that many persons, especially if they are young and not themselves the head of household, simply do not know what the income is.

Subject to the qualifications and interpretations above, a general pattern emerges from the survey results in east and south Los

Angeles. In both areas unemployment in the youth labor market had reached disastrous proportions in mid–1971. Chicano youngsters participate in the labor force to a greater degree than do Blacks, but neither group is particularly successful in obtaining jobs above the service, unskilled, low-level clerical, or semiskilled levels.[19] Educational attainment (quantitatively measured) is below average for both groups, more so for the Black than for the Chicano teenagers in our sample. Family income is low in both groups, though noticeably lower in Watts than in east Los Angeles. More than a third of the households in our Watts sample appear to be below the poverty line.

Whatever problems may arise indirectly from the *past* residence of parents, relatives, and associates in other areas, there is no evidence that migration from other states or from foreign countries is of any importance in the groups studied or has any direct impact on their educational or economic status. To the contrary, almost all interviewees have lived in Los Angeles County for long periods. What *does* appear to be a problem of some magnitude—notably so in Watts, but of greater significance in east Los Angeles than anticipated—is the degree of family disorganization reflected in numbers of households headed by someone other than the father. As argued later, this problem is of special meaning in relation to labor market entry and career choice because, typically, youngsters in all areas and ethnic groups receive much of their information, guidance, and labor force orientation from their fathers.

Whatever dubious merit the argument may have in other areas of the city, certainly it cannot be argued that, in communities like Watts and east Los Angeles, high rates of youth unemployment are really not critical because teenagers usually are not heads of households, and any income from employment is merely supplementary to the earnings provided by the head of household, normally an adult male. Aside from welfare allowances, or occasional earnings by a female head of household from low-paid employment, the income provided by teenagers or young adults is frequently the *only* income received by the household. Our survey shows that high percentages of the youngsters are themselves the heads of households (though relatively few report themselves as being married). Even in those cases where there is another adult male as head of household, the family income appears to be

## Table 1.

*Head of Household by Age and Area (Percent)*

| Age | South Los Angeles | | East Los Angeles | |
|---|---|---|---|---|
| | 16–19 | 20–24 | 16–19 | 20–24 |
| Person answering | 8.2 | 63.9 | 5.2 | 44.0 |
| Father | 40.3 | 17.0 | 67.4 | 33.0 |
| Mother | 41.0 | 15.6 | 22.1 | 15.4 |
| Brother or sister | 2.2 | 1.4 | 1.2 | 2.2 |
| Other relative | 1.5 | 1.4 | 2.9 | 3.3 |
| Someone else | 6.7 | 0.7 | 1.2 | 2.2 |

## Table 2.

*Labor Force Status, by Age and Area (Percent)*

| Age | South Los Angeles | | East Los Angeles | |
|---|---|---|---|---|
| | 16–19 | 20–24 | 16–19 | 20–24 |
| Working | 11.1 | 26.2 | 37.1 | 48.9 |
| Had job but not at work | 0.0 | 3.4 | 4.8 | 3.3 |
| Looking for work (unemployed) | 23.8 | 34.5 | 22.2 | 18.9 |
| Going to school (at survey time) | 57.1 | 20.7 | 15.6 | 6.7 |
| Unable to work | 4.0 | 5.5 | 5.4 | 4.4 |
| Other | 0.8 | 6.2 | 14.4 | 14.4 |
| Both working and going to school | 3.2 | 3.4 | 0.6 | 3.3 |

Note: Responses, as coded above, were in answer to the question: "What were you doing most of last week?"

## Table 3.

*Highest Grade Completed, Persons Not in School, by Age and Area (Percent)*

| Age | South Los Angeles | | East Los Angeles | |
|---|---|---|---|---|
| | 16–19 | 20–24 | 16–19 | 20–24 |
| 9th grade | 3.7 | 2.2 | 1.6 | 0.0 |
| 10th grade | 9.3 | 5.4 | 14.1 | 4.6 |
| 11th grade | 40.7 | 14.0 | 17.2 | 27.7 |
| 12th grade | 40.7 | 52.7 | 60.9 | 40.0 |
| 1st year of college | 5.6 | 9.7 | 6.3 | 9.2 |
| 2nd year of college | 0.0 | 7.5 | 0.0 | 13.8 |
| 3rd year of college | 0.0 | 4.3 | 0.0 | 1.5 |
| 4th year of college | 0.0 | 2.2 | 0.0 | 1.5 |
| Any other | 0.0 | 2.2 | 0.0 | 1.5 |

significantly below average, pervasively so in the Watts community.

Our exclusion of young women from this particular study does not reflect male chauvinism, but rather the exigencies of time and resources. It would have been impossible to gather a sufficient sampling of women to enable us to draw valid conclusions. We did in fact secure interviews with approximately a hundred women, but the size and nature of this sample would not allow us to do more than make a superficial and limited analysis; cross tabulations and more refined examination of results would be out of the question. I hope, sometime in the future, to expand on this base and conduct an adequate study of the career goals of young women.

There is, perhaps, a stronger reason for concentrating at this moment on the labor market experiences of young men. I am especially concerned with some economic aspects of the subeconomy in the ghetto and barrio, and on the whole, the males are more active in this informal economy than are the females. I do not deny that young women will participate in some degree, but my observations suggest that the street economy is more related to the activity and perceptions of men. After all, the existing welfare system is fashioned to provide income, albeit inadequate, to women in broken homes. In a sense, as I shall demonstrate later, the subeconomy is largely an unofficial form of welfare for the men who are otherwise denied access to a sufficient legal income.

Furthermore, the prevailing economic and social structure rests on an assumption that the basic and most pervasive income–receiving unit will remain the household headed by a man in the labor market. This may well change, as women secure meaningful equal rights and continue to enter the market in greater numbers, but as of now it is a fact to be reckoned with. Thus the most *urgent* need is to provide employment to young men who now live in low-income households. It is posited that welfare reform, however useful and helpful that may be in other ways, will do relatively little in and of itself to solve the problem of wasted and unrealized talent among the young men in Watts and east Los Angeles and comparable neighborhoods throughout the country. Other social goals, such as the restoration or maintenance of reasonable family stability, can hardly be considered attainable in the absence of some longer-run assurance of employment and advancement opportunity for the "dudes" on the street. This our society has so far failed to provide, and the consequences of that failure are everywhere visible.

Before proceeding to an examination of our survey findings, however, we should give some consideration to the existing theoretical and empirical explanations of youth unemployment, the factors which influence the allocation of young people among "alternative uses," and the determinants of career preference. The next chapter offers a review of the relevant literature.

NOTES

1. Figures are drawn from the U. S. Department of Labor's *Report on Manpower Requirements, Resources, Utilization, and Training,* included as part of the *Manpower Report of the President, 1971.* It should be noted that unemployment figures for nonwhite teenage *girls* are even higher, but for reasons discussed in the text this study focuses principally on the labor market experiences of young men.

2. *Current Population Reports*, Series P-20, No. 224, October 1971, "Selected Characteristics of Persons and Families of Mexican, Puerto Rican and Other Spanish Origin: March 1971," p. 10.

3. *Ibid.* The corresponding rate was 25.4 percent for Puerto Rican youngsters, the highest rate in any category listed.

4. *Current Population Reports*, Series P-20, No. 213, February 1971, "Persons of Spanish Origin in the United States: November 1969," p. 28.

5. Deborah P. Klein, "Determining the Labor Force Status of Men Missed in the Census," *Monthly Labor Review,* March 1970, p. 26. It should again be noted that the Census Bureau designates most Mexican Americans and Puerto Ricans as "white," which may mean that many of the uncounted whites fall into these "minority" categories.

6. *Ibid.*, pp. 27-32.

7. *America's Uncounted People*, Report of the Advisory Committee on Problems of Census Enumeration, Division of Behavioral Sciences, National Research Council, National Academy of Sciences, 1971, p. 3.

8. *Ibid.*, p. 32.

9. *Ibid.*, p. 91.

10. *Ibid.*, pp. 86-87.

11. One such example, among many, is the sharp divergence between the estimates of ghetto unemployment in Los Angeles, made by the McCone Commission in late 1965, and the figures produced by a special census in November of that year. As early as 1964 a report submitted by the staff of the UCLA Institute of Industrial Relations to the U.S. Department of Commerce stated: "The startling fact about the hard-core unemployed in the central city is that so many of them vanish from sight so quickly and so completely. . . . Public and private agencies reach only a proportion of the long term unemployed men. Also of probable significance is the income obtained, in varying amounts, from activities classified as illegal or illicit by society: gambling, 'numbers,' dope pushing, prostitution, theft, and so forth. . . ." *Hard-Core Unemployment and Poverty in Los*

*Angeles*, Washington, D.C.: Government Printing Office, 1965, pp. 236-237.

12. Most welfare assistance in this country has been directed to the *female* heads of households. However, high proportions of those already eligible for relief often do not receive it, for one reason or another. A study in New York's Lower East Side, conducted in 1960 by Professor Richard Cloward, revealed that approximately half of the area's eligible population was not on the relief rolls. See Frances Fox Piven and Richard A Cloward, *Regulating the Poor: The Functions of Public Welfare*, New York: Pantheon Books, 1971, p. 219.

13. *Manpower Report of the President, 1971*, pp. 98-99. A fuller account of this and other studies, and a summary of my own findings relative to the street economy, appear in Chapter 7.

14. The 1970 Census enumerated 1,289,311 Chicanos, or 18 percent of total population, and 762,844 Blacks, or 10 percent of the total, in Los Angeles County. As of this writing, census tract data had not yet been released, and generalizations about population distributions *within* the city and county are therefore based upon earlier estimates, such as an estimate made by the County Commission on Human Relations as of October 1967.

15. See, e.g., Bureau of Labor Statistics (BLS) Regional Report No. 14, Pacific Regional Office, pp. 6-8, for summary of unemployment figures from the July 1968—June 1969 UES results. Unemployment rates for teenagers (both sexes) were about 16 percent for Mexican Americans and 43 percent for Blacks, at that time.

16. This fact, emerging as it does from a survey taken in the midst of a severe recession, suggests some interesting possibilities that will be explored in later chapters.

17. Other surveys in Los Angeles and elsewhere suggest that the Chicanos usually have higher dropout percentages than do the Blacks. Our respective figures for Chicano and Black young adults are in line with this general finding, while our statistics for the teenagers might indicate that our Chicano interviewees in this age category are better off than the average. The apparently below-average percentage of dropouts among young adults surveyed in south Los Angeles may reflect a sampling bias introduced by the fact that many interviews in this age group were conducted by three young men who are themselves graduates of Jordan High School. They may have tended to interview a disproportionate number of classmates who, like themselves, were more likely to be graduates than dropouts.

18. The fact that incomes are generally higher in the predominantly Chicano than in the predominantly Black area corresponds as a pattern with the findings of other surveys and studies (for example, the 1968-1969 NES study mentioned before), but there is reason to believe that the difference is not as marked as the above statistics might suggest. For one thing, there was an extraordinarily high nonresponse rate to this question in east Los Angeles: 111 nonresponses out of a total of 268 interviews. It is perhaps reasonable to infer that a high percentage of nonrespondents will tend to fall in the lower income brackets. Furthermore, the responses to this question will be influenced by the fact that the interviewees were teenagers or young adults and often do not know precisely, or even approximately, what the actual family income is. In both areas the interviewers were instructed to *estimate* (on the basis of knowledge about

whether the respondent lived in public housing or was in a "welfare" family or other circumstances) whether the family income was below $4000 a year, between $4000 and $6000, or above $6000, without necessarily asking the question directly. In many instances, however, they asked the interviewee to check the appropriate category.

19. Chicanos penetrate semiskilled jobs to a greater degree than Blacks, and are somewhat more successful at the skilled level, but generally both groups are heavily concentrated in the lower skill categories.

# 2

---

# THE YOUTH LABOR MARKET:
# AN OVERVIEW

The employment problems of teenagers and young adults have received considerable attention from economists and sociologists in recent years, though much of it has been theoretical and speculative rather than empirical. Even the more empirically oriented studies, of course, have been handicapped by their inevitable reliance upon the available statistical data and the traditional techniques of social research, many of them deficient for the reasons suggested previously and demonstrated subsequently in this study. At the risk of some taxonomic oversimplification, it would appear that the various explanations of excessive unemployment or underemployment among young people (notably, *minority youngsters*) can be classified thus:

(1) Primarily economic and market-oriented interpretations based upon textbook descriptions of labor market behavior and supply and demand theory, focusing the blame largely on federally enforced minimum wages and other interferences with the freely competitive economy;

(2) A more "institutional" analysis emphasizing structural fac-

tors such as discrimination, educational and training problems, defective or inadequate processes of labor market information, transportation in relation to job and residential locations, and so forth, with these structural problems exacerbated at times by macroeconomic policies which unduly restrict economic growth and aggregate employment (often in the interest of controlling price inflation); and

(3) "Cultural" explanations which stress conflicts between the life style of the minority poor and that of the majority (including, most critically, the typical employers of labor). Analyses of this approach to the question may be found in the works of sociologists Oscar Lewis and Lee Rainwater, and in the most extreme and controversial form, in a recent book by political scientist Edward C. Banfield, entitled *The Unheavenly City.*

Whatever the premises of the respective theories, presumably all would share a common conclusion that investments in human capital—primarily via improved education and training—must enhance the labor market prospects of young people through a resulting increase in their productivity. "Productivity," variously defined, is the most generally recognized basis for determining the market worth of any worker. The forces which influence the productivity of young workers, and thus their employability, are reflected in both the labor supply and labor demand sides of the market: their own characteristics as individuals (level of education and skill, etc.) and the consumer demand and/or technological factors which influence the hiring decisions of potential employers. Wherever the level and distribution of employment are determined mainly by profit-maximizing employers responding to consumer choices in the competitive market, the income of every worker (young or old) will correspond with his or her productivity.

When noneconomic, or nonjob related, considerations enter the picture, some element of indeterminacy may result.[1] If either the employer or the jobseeker is influenced by conceptions of "job stigma" or feelings of "prejudice," he may not behave rationally in strictly economic terms. Neither may, in fact, maximize the quantitatively measurable returns from the market use of his resources. In a free society, of course, he is entitled to adopt any maximization principle he chooses, and he may choose to pursue goals which are inconsistent with the personal optimization of his productivity or his profit in the market. Thus the "hippie" with a college degree may choose to work as a dishwasher or bum around the country rather than become an executive (if a job were available) even though he might be better qualified than the crewcut WASP who is actually hired. The orthodox economist can only respond that, by so doing, he is not contributing to maximum output, income, and economic efficiency.

The above reasoning, in a sense, fuses the economic and cultural explanations of youth unemployment. The imperfections in the labor market can arise from diverse sources: government legislation, labor union policies, lack of accurate information on the part of jobseekers or employers, or cultural and institutional barriers. If anyone has full and accurate knowledge of alternative jobs and, for cultural reasons, does not make himself available for employment *on terms satisfactory to the employer*, to that degree his ensuing unemployment or underemployment must be regarded as "voluntary" rather than "involuntary." If he is available for work but simply lacks knowledge of its existence or of the means by which he can qualify himself for it, he is involuntarily unemployed because of a major structural defect in the labor market. If he is unable to find employment on any terms whatsoever (a possibility long denied by the classical economists), his involuntary unemployment is due to a major deficiency in aggregate demand. If jobs are not available to him because legislation or union policies or other interferences with competition prevent employers from offering work *on terms satisfactory to them*, his unemployment is involuntary to the extent that he would have accepted such employment had it been available. As a prelude to the empirical studies of the youth labor market which will follow, a brief overview of these theories is in order.

## The Impact of Minimum Wages

Perhaps the strongest and most unqualified case against minimum wage legislation has been stated by Professor Milton Friedman: "Women, teenagers, Negroes, and particularly Negro teenagers will be especially hard hit [by a 1966 law increasing the minimum wage from $1.25 to $1.60 per hour.] I am convinced that the minimum wage law is the most anti-Negro law on our statute books—in its effect not its intent."[2] These groups, he argued, are unskilled and relatively unproductive, and the denial of low-paid jobs to them also denies them the opportunity to obtain on-the-job training which is the main route to higher productivity and advancement. "It has always been a mystery to me to understand why a youngster is better off unemployed at $1.60 an hour than employed at $1.25."[3] He predicted a rise in the teenage unemployment rate to 30 percent as a result of the 1966 act.

Friedman even summons, as a witness for his case, an eminent Keynesian economist, Professor James Tobin of Yale University, who is quoted to the effect that: "People who lack the capacity to earn a decent living need to be helped, but they will not be helped by minimum wage laws, trade union wage pressures or other devices which seek to compel employers to pay them more than their work is worth. The more likely outcome of such regulations is that the intended beneficiaries are not employed at all."[4]

In another, more extended work, Professor Friedman reiterates these arguments and adds that those who are hurt by minimum wage laws "are anonymous and their problem is not clearly connected to its cause: the people who join the ranks of the unemployed or, more likely, are never employed in particular activities because of the existence of the minimum wage law and are driven to *even less remunerative* activities or to the relief rolls" (emphasis added).[5]

Additional support for Professor Friedman's position comes from a distinguished "New Economist," Professor Paul A. Samuelson, who asserts in his widely used textbook that government interferences in the labor market through minimum wage legislation "often hurt those they are designed to help. What good does it do a black youth to know that an employer must pay him $1.60 per hour if the fact that he must be paid that amount is what keeps him from getting a job?"[6] Through a graphic illustration, Professor Samuelson demonstrates that the setting of a minimum wage above the free market wage level forces an equilibrium at a wage which increases unemployment.

Recent statistical and empirical analysis of this theory fails to support it, though the findings are hardly conclusive. Comprehensive studies commissioned by the U. S. Department of Labor suggest that there is no clear-cut relationship between minimum wages and youth employment. There is some evidence that minimum wage legislation may have had somewhat adverse effects upon 16- and 17-year-old employment, particularly among students "who were Negroes and had limited labor market information, and among those students employed as service workers."[7] The general conclusion was that there is no support for a finding that the 1967 rise in minimum wages created relatively more unemployment among low-wage young workers. "The magnitude of the employment effects of minimum wage legislation probably has been small, as the studies included in this report underline, and consequently difficult to measure precisely."[8] The employment effects of minimum wage legislation, furthermore, may have been disguised by other economic forces operating at the same time, including youth employment generated by special federal manpower programs such as the Neighborhood Youth Corps and the Job Corps.

Under any circumstances, economists generally favor approaches to the problem of youth unemployment and low income which do not involve the direct fixing of wages or the setting of a wage floor. Their proposed solutions fall into three broad (and complementary) categories: (1) a subsidy in the form of income payments directly to those whose low productivity in the market denies them an income above the poverty level; (2) programs to enhance the productivity of "unskilled" persons by investments in human capital; and (3) efforts to remove or mitigate existing imperfections in the labor market through greatly improved processes of information, job data banks, new transportation facilities, increased labor mobility both spatially and occupationally, and elimination of racial discrimination and similar "nonperformance-related" barriers to employment. Some economists call for programs of deliberate job creation, primarily in the public sector, but the more orthodox economists such as Professor Friedman would deplore such action for the same reasons they oppose minimum wages: because it would involve a departure from the conventional labor market processes by which jobs are created and destroyed. The importance given by economists of diverse viewpoints to structural factors and investment in human capital suggests that a consideration of such issues, particularly in relation to the youth labor market, is next in order.

## Improvement in the Labor Market
## and Youth Productivity

Even the economists who are committed to competitive theory will avow that there are imperfections in the labor market, stemming from lack of information on the part of jobseekers and employers; immobility associated with housing segregation, inadequate transportation, and psychological or cultural ties with a particular neighborhood or work environment; racial discrimination; union policies, licensing and other governmental requirements, and similar factors which may restrict entry into given occupations or professions; and other barriers to the free movement of workers among alternative jobs in accordance with productivity and market demand. Presumably, some of these problems can be remedied or alleviated through enlightened social policy.

On the other hand, some degree of "frictional" unemployment is often regarded as salutary, in terms of the most productive allocation of labor. Professors Armen Alchian and William E. Allen, for example, point out that job changing and intermittent unemployment are natural characteristics of a volatile, free labor market, where (as in 1966) approximately ten million people change jobs or take new jobs during a year. "There is a persistent and extensive flow of people from job to job and between jobs and unemployment, along with constant reassessment of old jobs and consideration of possible new occupations."[9] It is important that those seeking new jobs acquire sufficient information about the alternatives, rather than taking the first available job. But information is not free or complete: some cost in resources and longer unemployment will often be required to acquire the needed information. Some unemployment is desirable because it permits more shopping around for the best available employment. "An essential function of the market is to make information about changing demands and supplies more readily (cheaply) accessible. Accepting the first offer reduces the probability of getting the highest paid job and lowers one's wealth (present value of his future earnings) compared to what it would be if he took longer to find more offers."[10]

Of course, Professors Alchian and Allen strongly adhere to the orthodox theory of labor market behavior, based upon a premise that "there are always jobs available if the wage rate is low enough."[11] Making information more conveniently accessible and more widely known is an appropriate way to improve the operation of the market, but minimum wages destroy employment for the unskilled and some job development policies aimed at keeping everyone employed will interfere with efficiency of job assignments, through arbitrary work assignments which are really "disguised unemployment."[12]

If labor market information is incomplete and imperfect under reasonably "normal" conditions, its inadequacy is heightened in those circumstances involving persons of low productivity and low levels of education. In the Black and Brown inner-city ghettos, the usual deficiencies in the information process are aggravated by at least three additional factors:

(1) Because much of the information about job opportunities usually comes through informal channels (such as tips or advice from a parent, another relative, or a friend), many youngsters in the low-income ghetto are at a disadvantage due to the fact that the other members of their household and their neighbors and friends are also likely to be unemployed or underemployed or out of the labor force, and therefore not in contact with firms which have job openings.

(2) Particularly in the Black ghetto, the father may be missing from the household and therefore the young male does not even have ready access to guidance or information (or mere example) which otherwise could be provided by an adult male head of household.

(3) The Black youngster (and, to a somewhat lesser degree, the Chicano youngster) typically lives in a segregated inner-city community which often is distant and isolated from major centers of employment, and especially in a large area like Los Angeles, the combination of housing segregation and deficient or unavailable transportation will mean that he is further cut off from sources of job information and, in many cases, from the job themselves.

The results of such problems have been well delineated by Professor Eli Ginzberg and his associates in the Conservation of Human Resources Project at Columbia University:

Most young entry workers begin with only a general notion of the kind of job they are seeking. Those with specific preemployment training, high school girls with clerical skills, apprentices, and the graduates of two or four year training programs have a better defined field of operation, but even they are often unaware of the nuances of difference among possible sites of employment. Nevertheless, their training makes it easier to use the organized placement services.

For the untrained, the information network on unemployment opportunity has serious defects. For the most part, it has negative characteristics—it is not a net and it does not work. The labor market is not a bourse where standard units are traded, nor do most job seekers engage in a systematic search. In New York as elsewhere, most information comes from one's family and circle of acquaintances. The less desirable the young worker on the basis of conventional criteria, the more important is the specific help available through the family. But, by and large, the amount of help available from one's family is usually in inverse proportion to the need. Negro boys in the ghetto, for example, seldom have alternate opportunities or personal intervention on their behalf.[13]

This analysis of labor market information deficiencies in the urban ghetto is shared by Professor Peter Doeringer of Harvard University, whose perceptive paper in the Proceedings of the December 1968 meeting of the Industrial Relations Research Association displays a greater awareness of the informal and unofficial forces affecting ghetto youth employment than do most other discussions of this issue: "There are persuasive *a priori* arguments for believing that information systems in the ghetto labor market operate less satisfactorily than those in the urban labor market as a whole. Numerous studies have demonstrated the importance of friends and relatives as a source of employment information, especially for low skilled jobs. In the ghetto, lower employment rates and skewed employment patterns tend to limit the quantity and quality of job information available to such a system, while increasing the demands placed upon it."[14]

One consequence is that young Blacks and Browns in the inner city must rely relatively more upon the public employment services and the schools as sources of labor market information, but these have proved to be of limited value. Little information of any worth is provided through the schools: in Los Angeles, for instance, the required tenth grade guidance class, lasting ten weeks, is on a parity with driver education and, aside from standard tests, is largely devoted to introducing the new student to high school. Almost no career and vocational data are imparted to youngsters in the ghetto and barrio schools, except occasionally and often accidentally on a hit-or-miss basis.

Even the system of nationally funded public employment exchanges is a relatively new phenomenon in the United States, from a historical perspective. Growing out of the Wagner-Peyser Act of 1933 and the personal leadership of Secretary of Labor Frances Perkins in the Roosevelt Administration, the Employment Service for many years suffered from its identification (in the eyes of most workers and employers) as the "unemployment service," which was primarily responsible for handing out unemployment compensation benefits. This confused but pervasive conception of its function was partially offset in the early 1960s by the physical separation of the Unemployment Insurance and Employment Service offices, but until recently the Employment Service has had the reputation of being *employer-* rather than *employee*-oriented, in the sense that it appeared more concerned with meeting the requirements of employers seeking workers than serving the interests of jobseekers.

Legislative and policy changes wrought by the manpower bills of recent years, beginning particularly with the original Manpower Development and Training Act of 1962, have fundamentally affected the functions of the Employment Service. Virtually every major legislative enactment in the manpower field has given the Employment Service a vital role in the recruitment and placement of trainees, most notably the young trainees. Thus the Service has become responsible for implementation of manpower legislation directed to the unemployed and underemployed (and even, at least ostensibly, the "hard core"). Reorganization of the public employment services, with the old Bureau of Employment Security having been dissolved and replaced in part by the new U. S. Training and Employment Service, has further strengthened their role in relation to the problems of unemployed or underemployed youngsters in big-city ghettos and barrios.[15] Despite these moves, the image of the Service in the eyes of those young people remains essentially negative, and the amount of tangible assistance reported by them is minimal.

Obviously, better counseling and a more efficient flow of labor market information cannot solve the more basic problems afflicting young men and women whose productivity in market terms is low and for whom there are no available jobs at decent wages. Much of the thrust of manpower legislation, therefore, has been directed toward two corollary goals: (1) increasing their productivity through vocational training and general education, and (2) encouraging employers, both private and public, to hire the young without discrimination based on race or national origin, age or other factors unrelated to job performance. The Nixon Administration has given particular emphasis to the JOBS program under which private employers receive subsidies from the federal government to cover a major part of the training and initial wage costs of hiring "disadvantaged" workers (including, of course, the minority young) and training them on the job. This represents some shift in emphasis away from the "institutional" (classroom) training often provided in MDTA programs. Again, the observed effects of subsidized on-the-job training in areas such as Watts and east Los Angeles, as reported by young men, continue to be almost nonexistent.

There have been, in addition, limited and seemingly desultory efforts to create additional employment for the so-called hard core, with some emphasis on job creation for youngsters in the minority areas. The recent Public Service Careers program is an example of this thrust, but at best it remains a severely restricted approach to the massive problem of minority youth unemployment or misemployment. Meaningful job creation on an extensive scale has not been attempted, partly because it is expensive and government has been unwilling to undertake it (particularly in the face of inflationary pressures) and partly because it runs counter to the strong beliefs of most economists, who prefer that the allocation of manpower remain strictly a function of the private competitive market.

To most of the Watts and east Los Angeles youngsters, "job creation" has been synonymous with the Neighborhood Youth Corps (NYC). Many of them have participated in the NYC program (in Watts, these jobs often are provided through the Watts Labor Community Action Committee), but they report that the jobs generally are in the custodial, maintenance, and low-level clerical fields and, apparently, very little useful on-the-job training is offered. Indeed, it appears that many NYC and similar jobs have little content and primarily serve as excuses for the payment of small amounts of money to young people in poverty neighborhoods. This, at least, seems to be the perception of many youngsters.

In this sense much NYC employment may actually be "disguised unemployment" (as defined earlier by Professors Alchian and Allen). Professor Charles C. Killingsworth of Michigan State University, a leading exponent of the "structural" explanation of unemployment as opposed to the "transitional" school, has noted in congressional testimony that a 1965 change in the definition of unemployment, which thereby included NYC and similar workers either as "employed" or "out of the labor market" rather than "unemployed," has significantly reduced the reported unemployment rates for young people and has therefore hidden large amounts of persistent joblessness. He points out that these programs which "hide" a great deal of structural unemployment have partly been responsible for oversanguine estimates of the effectiveness of fiscal and monetary policy in alleviating the overall problem of unemployment in the United States.[16]

Even those economists who adhere to fiscal and/or monetary explanations of excessive unemployment, and therefore oppose the "structural" analysis, concede that unemployment rates in the minority youth labor markets have been resistant to the presumed effects of liberal fiscal or monetary policies. Quoting "New Economist" Walter Heller to the effect that unemployment in general can be more easily explained in fiscal than in structural terms, Professor Samuelson notes that Negro unemployment, especially among young people, has remained high relative to white unemployment in all years studied, regardless of changes in the level of aggregate demand. This suggests that structural factors may be at work, at least in minority areas. He concludes that "Much research is needed here."[17]

## Youth Unemployment as a "Cultural" Phenomenon

In the eyes of some analysts, the main structural factor behind persisting unemployment in low-income areas is cultural in origin. In their view much unemployment persists because the "lower class" culture conflicts with the needs and demands of employers and many members of that class (particularly among young people) reject the work ethic and are present rather than future oriented. There is disagreement among sociologists and cultural anthropologists as to whether the economic behavior of the poor, especially the *minority* poor, is the result of a distinctive "culture of poverty" or whether it is predominantly adaptive in nature. If it is the latter, presumably the poor behave as they do because they are denied an effective opportunity to behave otherwise. In this case the basic goals of the poor and the better off are perceived as essentially the same, but there are differences in their respective abilities or opportunities to achieve those goals. As Ernest Hemingway once remarked to F. Scott Fitzgerald in a well-quoted conversation, the rich are different from everyone else because they have more money.

Some ramifications of this dispute are beyond the scope of this study, but its general relationship to the question of youth unemployment should be obvious. If young men in urban slums (and in higher income communities too) are not achievement oriented and not interested in a career, by definition they cannot succeed in a market economy based upon work orientation and their resistance to proferred employment, *even at extremely low wages*, must be regarded as socially pathological.

The most extreme advocate of this view is Professor Edward Banfield of Harvard University, whose book *The Unheavenly City* is probably the purest example of twentieth-century Social Darwinism now extant.[18] Arguing, in substance, that Black and Chicano youngsters in the inner-city ghetto are burdened not by racial discrimination or any lack of opportunity, but rather by their own personal and cultural defects, he attributes much of their unemployment to their pathological "present mindedness" and refusal to accept employment on terms which low wage employers can afford. Their tendency to refuse such employment and "get away with it" is supported, and to some extent suborned, by presumably misguided government policies which denigrate the low-wage employer and compel him to pay an unskilled worker a higher wage than he is willing and able to pay; by social and political beliefs that there should be a minimum income standard for everyone; and by alternative sources of income from social welfare or from illicit economic activity in the streets. In his discussion of unemployment, Banfield concludes:

Even if there were a lively demand at high wages for all the labor in the city, however unproductive, some people would remain unemployed. Members of the lower class work only intermittently even if job opportunities are good. Providing for a future, even a week or two away, is not part of their culture; nor will they accept the discipline that a job usually imposes. Youth culture somewhat resembles lower class culture in these respects. Teenage boys are often strongly disinclined to work; they like to be "where the action is." Jobs that are lawful, safe, and well regulated are often more than they can stand—especially if they do not pay well. And in an ever more affluent society, those who prefer to live from hand to mouth without working find it increasingly easy to do so.[19]

In arguing that there is an informal wage minimum set by peer group standards and public opinion, Banfield also recognizes the impact of illegal sources of income. "Illicit enterprises, too, tend to have the effect of setting an informal minimum wage for unskilled labor that has no relation to the market value of such labor and that other employers cannot afford to pay. As a result, the young dropout loses face and self-respect unless he is either a 'hustler' or an idler; the suggestion that he be paid what his work is worth is tantamount to an insult."[20] He finds support for this view in the statement (quoted from another study) of a Harlem youngster, to the effect that the young man can "make $40 to $50 a day selling marijuana" and that therefore there is no point in his going to the garment district for a job which might produce $40 or $50 *a week* "if I'm lucky."[21]

In his recommendations for action, Banfield prefers policies which remove any legal restrictions (such as minimum wages) on low-wage employers, institutionalize the "incompetent poor" (encompassing much of what he describes as the lower class) either by encouragement or by force, subsidize the "competent poor" at a poverty income level by paying income supplements to the low wages they receive in the marketplace, and regulate the lower class rigidly by establishing a virtual police state in low-income communities. The lower class would be pressured to adopt the "normal" culture and abandon its own as quickly and completely as possible, and would suffer severe social penalties if it resisted.[22] He regretfully admits that his recommendations are politically unacceptable.

Professor Banfield takes care to emphasize that his remarks are directed at *class* rather than *racial* behavior, and he denies that the question of race per se is relevant to urban problems. It is clear that the Black "lower class" is, in fact, a particular target, but even in strictly class terms his views and analysis are not shared by many sociologists and anthropologists. They regard "lower class" behavior, irrespective of race, as a functional adaptation to conditions in which members of this class live, rather than as a cultural deviance from and defiance of the major values and norms of the popular majority. Thus they do not view "lower class" life styles as pathological (as does Banfield), and some analysts find positive behavioral characteristics among the lower-class poor: a greater capacity to express spontaneous warmth and affection, love of children, "egalitarianism, informality and humor," and many other affirmative traits.[23] The case for the "adaptational" school has been stated by Professor Hylan Lewis:

> The behavior of the bulk of the poor Negro families appears as pragmatic adjustments to external and internal stresses and deprivations experienced in the quest for essentially common values. A seeming paradox is that affirmation of, if not demonstration of, some of America's traditional virtues and values in their purest form is found to be strong and recurrent among even the most deprived of Negro families. Our view is that it is probably more fruitful to think of different types of low-income Negro families reacting in various ways to the facts of their position and to relative isolation rather than to the imperatives of a lower-class or significantly different ethnic culture. It is important that we do not confuse the basic life chances and actual behavior of the contemporary Negro parent with his basic cultural values and preferences.

Our experience suggests further that the focus of efforts to change should be on background conditions and on precipitants of deviant behavior rather than on the presumably different class or cultural values operative in child-rearing behavior among Negroes, and particularly low income Negroes. The way to remove the threat of the problem behavior of low-income Negro families is not likely to be found in a kind of functionalism or cultural relativism, or in sealing off persons who are presumed to be most inclined to exhibit such behavior; nor is it to be found in getting low-income urban Negro families in general, or a segment of them, to revamp what is presumed to be their culture.[24]

The thrust of this argument, of course, is that the unemployment problems of Black and Chicano young men can be met by programs to expand employment (real employment, not "make work" which is dead end in nature) and to provide opportunities which will lead to improvement in their life chances. They are "alienated" only in the sense that they are continually frustrated in their efforts to achieve basically the same economic and social goals as are pursued by the majority of Anglos, not in the sense that they reject those goals and seek to pursue others. In arguing that the degree of value alienation is not as great or as significant in our society as many have assumed, Professor Melvin Seeman of UCLA finds that studies in Los Angeles show "a fairly high degree of agreement in values and attitudes across the major lines of cleavage that are so fundamental in our thinking about urban life: across race, sex, occupation, etc. To a degree that I certainly would not have expected, the blacks and whites, the manual and nonmanual workers, fathers and mothers, suburban and central city residents show little difference in their views concerning a wide range of issues—for example, the values they would like to see their children accomplish in life and in school; the importance of status striving for themselves; sentiments of generalized trust in others; preferences in family decision-making processes; commitments concerning conformity, materialism, the primacy of self-interest over social welfare; and the like."[25]

Certainly, in their own expressed views, the young men of Watts and east Los Angeles reflect no lack of interest in the material goals which are commonly pursued in American society. To the extent that their behavior in the street ("hustling," petty crime, gambling, etc.) seems to differ from the articulated norms of the majority, they justify it in terms of the necessity to *survive* and do not assign to it any inherently positive values. It may be ironic that, among the various segments of America's youth population, perhaps only the low-income minority youngsters suffer no guilt feelings whatsoever about pursuing materialistic goals—cars, good clothes, etc.

In a discussion of the ethics of stealing, several of the Watts teenagers agreed that it is justified only by the need to survive in a world where there seems to be little alternative at times: "I get tired of asking my mother for money" (Michael). "Like they always say, B— [a young friend] is bad. Still, you got to realize a lot of them have jobs and he hasn't. Like I said, he gets fifty cents a day and he go around with people that is employed for somebody and maybe three or four dollars run us a day, and he got fifty cents a day—how in the hell is he gonna keep up with us if nobody giving him nothing? He gonna get it—he's gonna get it some kind of way. I mean he could better himself, but would you give a child fifty cents a day to go out there on the street? And the street is hell and what do you think he's gonna do to rest and fifty cents ain't gonna last nowhere. I can't even get past women really with fifty cents. And I need a bill when I walk down the curb" (Robert). But the youngsters also agreed that stealing does not genuinely help in the long run, and for that matter neither does "getting high." One youngster remarked: "See, I'm trying to get over. I got it and realized that I cannot go on stealing, that I cannot go on trying to beat society, that is dead" (Robert). Another eloquently summarized his feelings: "Like me, like I had the problem of getting loaded, you know? I'm gonna tell you actually I felt like this and this is from my heart, like coming from the real side. How many brothers have been faced with the fact that you are in the home; you don't know how to righteously hustle. Still, carrying on ain't gonna put food in your mouth—you gonna be hungry, I know how it is to be hungry. I know how it is to be without a parent, I know how it is to be alone in the darkness—no water, no light. I'm not using this as an excuse for getting loaded."[26]

One theme running through all analyses of youth unemployment (with the possible exception of Professor Banfield's) is that the established labor market does not function efficiently in providing employment or labor market information to young persons who live in central-city ghettos, whatever their cultural preferences may be. Some important impacts of this deficiency are discussed in the following chapters.

NOTES

1. In purely theoretical terms, of course, the problem can be solved by translating the consideration into "opportunity cost" equivalents. Thus the

employer who exercises a "taste for discrimination" in racial terms thereby makes that consideration a part of his cost of doing business, perhaps even at the risk of failing to maximize his profit. In realistic terms, however, the presence of subjective or sociological factors as influences upon economic decisions will often make it impossible to predict the outcome.

2. *Readings in Economics*, 6th ed., Paul A. Samuelson (ed.), New York: McGraw Hill, 1970, p. 247.

3. *Ibid.*, p. 247.

4. *Ibid.* It is noteworthy that nearly all economists, regardless of general philosophy, appear to look unfavorably on such measures as minimum wage laws, tariffs, and farm price supports. In the field of microeconomics, apparently they tend to accept the economic desirability of market pricing; their disagreements, it would seem, are more likely to be found in the macroeconomic field or in areas where the focus is not strictly economic or centered on questions of economic efficiency. John Kenneth Galbraith, of course, remains an exception to all such generalizations.

5. Milton Friedman, *Capitalism and Freedom*, Chicago: University of Chicago Press, 1962, p. 181.

6. Paul A. Samuelson, *Economics*, 8th ed., New York: McGraw-Hill, 1970, p. 372.

7. *Youth Unemployment and Minimum Wages,* Bulletin 1657, U.S. Department of Labor, Bureau of Labor Statistics, 1970, p. 183. Valuable papers and discussion on this same topic may be found in the *Proceedings of the 23rd Annual Winter Meeting*, Industrial Relations Research Association, December 28-29, 1970, pp. 106-144.

8. *Youth Unemployment and Minimum Wages,* p. 188.

9. Armen Alchian and William R. Allen, *University Economics*. Belmont, Calif.: Wadsworth Publishing Company, 1967, p. 495.

10. *Ibid.*, p. 500.

11. *Ibid.*, p. 496.

12. *Ibid.*, p. 507.

13. Eli Ginzberg and Associates, *Manpower Strategy for the Metropolis,* New York: Columbia University Press, 1968, pp. 141-142.

14. Peter B. Doeringer, "Manpower Programs for Ghetto Labor Markets," *Proceedings of the 21st Annual Winter Meeting*, Industrial Relations Research Association, December 29-30, 1968, p. 258.

15. The employment service section of the old BES has been combined with the Bureau of Work-Training Programs in the U.S. Department of Labor. The Training and Employment Service provides staff services to regional offices and to the various state agencies, and control of employment service offices remains primarily a state responsibility. For an analysis and recommendations for further improvement of public employment services, see the *Report to the Secretary of Labor from the Employment Service Task Force* (chaired by George P. Schultz), reprinted in *Toward a Manpower Policy*, Robert A. Gordon (ed.). New York: John Wiley, 1967, pp. 143-173.

16. Statement of Professor Killingsworth to the U. S. Senate Subcommittee on Employment, Manpower and Poverty, 1970, reprinted in *Rising Unemployment: A Transitional Problem?*, Research Reprint Series No. 122, 1970-1971, School of Labor and Industrial Relations, Michigan State University.

17. Paul A. Samuelson, *Economics*, 8th ed., New York: McGraw Hill, 1970, p. 802.

18. Boston: Little, Brown, 1968. The violence of his attack on the "lower class" and the repressive nature of his recommendations for its control have led some to speculate that Professor Banfield may be a satirist in the tradition of Jonathan Swift. It seems more likely, however, that he is dead serious and that his prescriptions for social policy stem from a fear of "lower class" (especially Black) violence which itself is pathological.

19. Edward Banfield, *The Unheavenly City*, Boston: Little, Brown, 1968, p. 112.

20. *Ibid.*, p. 101.

21. *Ibid.*, p. 101. It is worthy of note that the economic behavior described by the Harlem youngster is perfectly rational in terms of the consumer-oriented free market which Banfield elsewhere extols, though he obviously finds the behavior distasteful and unacceptable in *this* context. It would appear that Banfield approves the competitive market and "consumer sovereignty" only where they clearly benefit the upper class, never where they might economically benefit the lower. Further discussion of these points may be found in Chapter VII of this report.

22. *Ibid.*, pp. 244-246.

23. A useful summary of the views of this school, and of others, may be found in a paper by Professor Robert Brischetto of the University of Texas at El Paso, "Social Scientists' Views of Minority Group Life Styles: A Classification of Perspectives on Blacks and Chicanos," presented at the March 1971 meeting of the Southwestern Sociological Association, Dallas, Texas.

24. See Professor Lewis' chapter "Family Life among Low-Income Urban Negroes," in *Employment, Race, and Poverty*, Arthur M. Ross and Herbert Hill (eds.), New York: Harcourt, Brace & World, 1967, pp. 170-171. Professor Lee Rainwater is also a prominent and articulate spokesman for this general viewpoint: see "Crucible of Identity: The Negro Lower-Class Family," in *The Negro American*, Vol. 2, *Daedalus*, Winter 1966, pp. 172-216. The whole concept of a "culture of poverty" is a controversial one. Originally popularized by anthropologist Oscar Lewis, who observed similar cultural traits in the various poverty families he studied in the United States and in other countries, it has been vigorously attacked by others such as sociologist Lewis Coser. Coser, in a recent address to the American Sociological Association and an article published in the October 1971 issue of *Dissent*, criticizes the notion on grounds that it is based on an incorrect premise, unduly discourages attempts to abolish poverty through income redistribution, and sometimes tends to "romanticize" poverty. He thinks that poverty should be regarded as an unmitigated evil, to be eliminated totally, and that there is no such thing as a "culture of poverty" (whether defined positively or negatively). My own impression is that the young men in Watts and east Los Angeles would strongly agree with the observations of Coser. My further conclusion (which I believe they would also share) is that the abolition of poverty need *not* be accompanied by an abandonment of all the cultural traits associated with the members of low-income minority households. I have more to say about this in later chapters.

25. Melvin Seeman, "The Urban Alienations: Some Dubious Theses from Marx to Marcuse," *Journal of Personality and Social Psychology*, Vol.

19, No. 2, 1971, p. 141. Reprinted by Institute of Industrial Relations, UCLA, Reprint 220.

26. Unless otherwise indicated, all quotations from Watts or east Los Angeles youngsters are drawn from personal interviews conducted in conjunction with this study. Because illegal activities were sometimes discussed, or criticisms were often directed against teachers or administrators or policemen, I have used fictitious first names on occasion to identify the various interviewees. However, in the case of Alfred Jackson, an articulate young man whom I interviewed only on the subject of education and counseling, I have used his real name because there seems to be no valid reason for concealing his identity.

# 3

---

# COUNSELING AND
# THE SCHOOL EXPERIENCE

It is hardly news that the public schools provide little or nothing in the way of effective vocational guidance or career counseling. Nor is this deficiency limited to ghetto or barrio areas; there is no evidence that the schools in other, less deprived areas are significantly better in this field. The young man in Watts and east Los Angeles, however, is especially burdened by the absence of meaningful labor market information at the school level, because many of the channels available to youngsters in higher-income communities are closed to him, and his dependence upon public institutions is correspondingly greater. Furthermore, the *general* quality of the education received by him is likely to be lower than it is in the more privileged communities, leaving him with even more limited alternatives and prospects.

The young man in Watts is perhaps more burdened than his counterpart in east Los Angeles, though the degree of disenchantment with the school system as a whole seems about equal in the two areas. He is more likely to live in a broken home where the father is missing and a major source of advice and information on jobs is therefore unavailable, and because of more intense discrimination and other factors, his ability to penetrate the semiskilled and skilled job market is more impaired. On the other hand, the transiency and dropout rates in both areas are high and despite the higher economic status of their households and their better record in obtaining production jobs, the Chicano youngsters we surveyed remain concentrated in the lesser skilled occupations.

The Los Angeles District high schools have had a tenth grade guidance class for many years, serving twin functions of introducing the incoming freshmen to high school and offering some basic testing to ascertain aptitudes and interests. Though there are variations by school, in most cases less than half the time spent in the required ten-week course is devoted to testing and vocational information. In certain ghetto schools testing is not even provided because the reading and comprehension levels of students are considered so low that test results are thought to be meaningless. To the extent that our group of interviewees remembered the class at all, they recalled it as an "introduction to high school," offering information on school personnel and activities and so forth. They were far more likely to recall the driver education class which is given following guidance.[1]

Barely a third of our respondents in south Los Angeles could recall having taken this required class, and the pattern is essentially the same in east Los Angeles. Even students then in the tenth grade, where guidance is given, could not recall or identify the class which supposedly gave them career information. A typical comment by those who recalled it at all: "That [guidance] was just about the school. We went over a little of it [testing and vocational guidance], but not as much as I·think we should have. Basically they tell you who's the principal and V.P. and things like that, that's all it was about, it wasn't nothing" (Earl—east Los Angeles).

Naturally, the general awareness of aptitude testing and the impact of "career days" in the schools is no greater. As for individual counseling, it is widely regarded as a farce, with blatant favoritism shown to those students who please the teachers and administrators: "Very few of them [the teachers], what they'll do, they'll talk to the *better* student after class, you know, after school—have the better student come in and give him a little guidance then. They could look out the window and see a student who is not doing too good and say, 'Well, he's not going to amount to nothing,' and then don't even try to help him or anything, unless he comes to them. And then usually, if you come to a teacher, first thing you got to get over is the remarks they're going to make, like, 'You should have been doing this in class, but I'll try to help you,' stuff like that. Like they're doing me a big personal favor, when sometimes it's strictly the teacher's fault. Not that the guy can't know the stuff, but he's not in a way to keep up with the class. And so that's why the teacher might have three outstanding students, and so she'll try to keep the class up there with them. As far as this guy who is lagging behind, she don't bother with him" (Alfred Jackson).

"The school system—I mean the school they only take the people that have good grades, who like are on the honor society, people who are in organizations in school, those are the only people they take. They don't take people like us, who, for example, don't get involved in that, 'cause like really you can't relate to it. You know like me and him [another youngster] one time I hit him up—he doesn't like to participate in school activities—I just hit him up, you know, about this teen club. So we went over there, to one of their meetings; they was talking about the war, you know, Uncle Tom shit. They're in all the high class organizations, I mean what *they* consider high class. I don't know but to me it ain't nothing 'cause grades. I consider myself just as intelligent as those punks are, they're intelligent in their way about the government, you know, they're puppets, but so therefore I consider everybody in this room intelligent, but the school system says, 'you're a dumb dropout.' That is all the school system is. Like the people who drop out of school, you know that they righteously have the guts, the balls to do it, 'cause I guess they realize that this is a bunch of bull, they're going to say 'fuck it.' You know, I used to go to a counselor and ask him about graduation, and I would just sit there for an hour and then the bell would ring for lunch and they would never call me back" (Earl).

One of the major criticisms directed by young men against tenth grade guidance, aside from its lack of substance, is its placement so early in the high school curriculum. No student, they feel, has even a remote interest in the subject at that stage of his education, "because it's just like some of the kids in kindergarten—'if you do your lessons real good, when you get to the sixth grade you go to junior high school.' At that particular time, they're not worried about going to junior high school because they're just in kindergarten. Same way with that guidance class. What are you going to do, worry about three years from that particular day? Three years from then, you don't even hardly remember what they said—the stereotype thing like 'the good grade will get you a good job' " (Alfred Jackson).

On the surface there would appear to be some logic in placing guidance in the first semester of the tenth grade. Presumably the testing and discussions would be of future value to the student and his counselor in planning his academic program, and the labor market information would be useful to those who drop out without graduating. Placement in the twelfth grade would make it meaningless in these terms, despite the obvious advantage that those who had survived the three years of school would be more keenly interested in the subject matter at that point in their education.

Yet these goals are seldom reached in practice. To the extent that labor market information is conveyed at all, it is more likely to come from the vocational teachers on a hit or miss basis. Nor is there any evidence that counselors make frequent or significant use of test results from guidance in advising students academically. The students I interviewed and the counselors and teachers I surveyed tend to agree that there is little or no connection between the 10-week guidance course and the subsequent grade counseling of pupils. "That [guidance] was just a classroom. Like, all your counselor sees is your grade—he doesn't know maybe if you do take a test. I don't think he even knows about it"[2] (Donna—south Los Angeles).

The amount of contact students typically have with *vocational* counselors or "work experience coordinators" in the public schools seems to differ somewhat according to a number of variables: the economic status of households in the area (e.g., how many of them have incomes below the poverty line), the majors of students, and the program at the school. In south Los Angeles, for example, the interviewees who attended Jordan indicated relatively more contact than did those who attended Locke. One of the important reasons for this, it would appear, is that there are more "college prep" majors at Locke, and naturally they are primarily or exclusively interested in *academic* counseling. In addition, Jordan draws its students almost entirely from a very low income area, while the

Locke students tend to be somewhat better off as a group. The immediate need for work, therefore, is more desperate among Jordan students than among those at Locke, although family income is below standard in both groups.[3]

The amount of contact reported in east Los Angeles is even lower than it is in the Watts area. Whereas the students in Watts usually indicated that they knew at least to whom they would go for information and counseling on jobs, a slight majority of the east Los Angeles youngsters either did not know or were unsure. These results are again consistent with our thesis that the amount of contact with vocational counselors or "work experience coordinators" varies to some degree with the percentage of college prep majors and low-income households represented within the school population.[4]

The high dropout rates observed for these schools (in both east and south Los Angeles) in the late 1960s, contrasted with the lower rates in 1970 and particularly with the high *in*-school rate reported in our Watts area survey in mid-1971, suggest the possibility that there is an inverse correlation between the unemployment rate and the dropout rate in low-income areas. An expanding, high-employment economy tends to draw many youngsters out of school and into the labor market, while recession and joblessness have the opposite effect. The basic reasons are obvious: when work is available, even at low levels, the lure is strong and almost irresistible for young men from low-income households, for whom the school experience at best has been considerably less than satisfactory. When this attraction is absent, as it is in the depth of a recession (the word, of course, should be "depression" for the minority areas), there is far less motivation to leave school.

In addition, there are special circumstances in areas like east Los Angeles and Watts. Many schools make no attempt to retain pupils regarded as troublesome or unmotivated, and quite a few are sent from school to school on what is euphemistically termed the "opportunity transfer."[5] The student's decision to leave school and enter the labor market fulltime (or the subeconomy, for that matter) is not only tolerated but encouraged in such cases: "They just don't want me in east L.A. schools, 'cause I don't dig on school. If I go to another school they thought I was going to change, like I was going to study harder at some other school. It don't matter what school I go to, I just don't dig on school, period.

They just say 'opportunity,' but it's just like going to another school. You know, to make it sound better to parents they'll say it's 'opportunity,' but it's just like kicking you out" (Alex—east Los Angeles).

The disenchantment is mutual. With some exceptions the young people in south and east Los Angeles are articulately scornful of the value and quality of the education they receive, and will often assert that it makes no real difference whether they attend school or drop out. Many of them claim, for instance, that they stay in school mainly to please parents. The prospect of employment will strengthen their inclination to drop out; the unavailability of work on the outside will reinforce parental pressures to stay in. "I'm actually not missing anything" by missing school (Robert). Other comments show the same feelings: "It's screwed up now because if you goof off you're in a goof-off class and you don't learn nothing" (Gil—east Los Angeles). "I'm going to stay at Dorsey. They won't just let you graduate, you know, just to get you out. You do have to have a balance of credits under your major before you graduate" (Donna).

"See, the teacher in high school—well, they might tell you something, they are not going to explain it out to you. You have to figure it out for yourself" (Willard—south Los Angeles). "I'm just out with a high school diploma and I ain't got nothing yet. I didn't learn nothing from school, but I learned more from him and his brother [others in the room] and other people in the community than I did in school, so the education I have I got from the community, not from school" (Earl).

There are some reasons to believe that, at least in short run terms, their assessment has merit. For those who are not college-oriented and do not seek employment which normally requires a diploma or degree, it is not at all clear that staying in school significantly improves their labor market prospects. Assuming that entry-level jobs are available and employers are prepared to train for advancement on the job, the young man may do at least as well in the labor market without the diploma. Our survey findings tend to confirm that the dropouts in east Los Angeles and Watts do not fare much worse than those who graduate, in securing the types of jobs which may be available to young men in those communities. It is obvious, of course, that this is hardly the best *long-run* alternative for them, because it effectively bars them from the expanding professional, technical and higher-level service occupations. A great many employers, public and private, continue to use arbitrary and unvalidated job stipulations requiring diplomas, degrees, and other "credentials," often as a means of subtly screening out the applicants from minority communities.

On the other hand, the onset of economic recession closes off many of the channels of usual employment, even at the lower levels. At the same time some students will increasingly look to the school itself as a source of employment or financial aid, and particularly if he is regarded as a good student and potential college material, a young man may find that the administration is prepared to provide on-campus work or guide him into part-time off-campus employment in order to help him stay in school. Some of the group of interviewees were critical of the process by which such work is arranged and allocated, claiming that the school plays favorites and reserves its favors for those students who are most conformist and compliant rather than those who may be in greater need.

Our survey findings suggest that in such a recession period Chicano youngsters continue to penetrate the semiskilled occupations more successfully than do the Blacks, and this explains in part why they are more likely to enter the labor market while the Black teenagers attend school in a somewhat higher proportion. In both cases, however, the tendency to stay in school seems to be stronger in periods of recession than in periods of prosperity. The Blacks have an additional incentive to remain in school longer: according to our sample findings those in Watts receive proportionately more concrete assistance from the school in finding employment than do those in east Los Angeles.

Thus the young men in Watts, and to a somewhat lesser degree in east Los Angeles, receive little useful information or career counseling in high school and enter the labor market with minimal guidance from either school or home. Because of labor market discrimination, family disorganization, faulty early education, segregation, and related factors, these young men require relatively more assistance from government and the school than do the Anglos in higher-income communities. The evidence at hand demonstrates that the Anglos also receive little counseling of value from their schools: in a 1969 Connecticut school survey, it was found that two out of every three students indicating a need for

## Table 4.

*Summary of Questionnaire on Counseling and Guidance*

1. Do you have a  class  in guidance and career selection in your school?
   18  Yes    3  No

2. If so, approximately how much time in that class over its total length is devoted to aptitude testing and/or information on careers?

| | |
|---|---|
| 20% (2) | Approximately 60% (2) |
| 25% (1) | 10 hours during a 10 week course (1) |
| 30% (1) | 10 weeks (5–50 min. a week per student |
| 40% (2) |    (10th grade) (1) |
| 45% (2) | Depends upon the teacher (1) |
| 50% (2) | Some guidance and career planning takes place |
| Over 50% (3) |    in the Social Science classes (1) |
| | No answer (2) |

3. What sort of tests, if any, are administered to students in that class?

   | | |
   |---|---|
   | 12 | Kuder Preference Record |
   | 11 | Differential Aptitude Test |
   | 1 | Armed Services Aptitude Test |
   | 1 | Brainerd Interest Inventory |
   | 1 | Henman-Nelson |
   | 1 | Test of Academic Progress |
   | 1 | All required tests – State mandate |
   | 1 | None |
   | 3 | No answers |

4. Do you have an opportunity to discuss the test results  individually with students?   15  Yes    3  No    3  No answer

5. (To class instructors) In terms of its effectiveness in conveying useful career and labor-market information to students, how would you rate the guidance class?

   | | | | |
   |---|---|---|---|
   | 0 | Excellent | 2 | Poor |
   | 6 | Good | 6 | No answer |
   | 7 | Fair | | |

6. (To class instructors and head counselors) To your knowledge, how often are test results and other information from guidance class used in the grade counseling of individual students?

   | | | | |
   |---|---|---|---|
   | 2 | Always | 5 | Rarely |
   | 2 | Often | 0 | Never |
   | 9 | Occasionally | 3 | No answer |

7. Does your school have Career Days?   13  Yes   8  No

8. If so, how often and under what circumstances are they given?
   Once a year
   Once a year for seniors
   Once a year under the direction of a career advisor
   Annually given on Saturdays
   Each year until 1970
   Annually students are guests of businesses on voluntary basis
   Annually—one week long—to begin March 1972
   Annually at campus
   Once a year by the L.A. City Schools. Given at a centrally located
      area to which students are bused.
   We had a career day in 1969. I feel that career days tend to give
      superficial information on jobs and careers.
   Departmental/seniors/and participation in Annual Career Guidance
      Center sponsored by Los Angeles County Superintendent of Schools
   Since invitations to career days are a limited number (20–25), only
      1% can attend, but for those few it is beneficial
   Have had first one this semester. Will probably have one each semester
      since this was extremely effective.
   8 No answers

9. How would you rate attendance at Career Days?
   | 2 | Excellent | 2 | Fair |
   | 8 | Good | 9 | Poor |

10. If the guidance class has an instructional manual and reading list,
    how often are they revised and updated?

    No manual available
    Infrequently (2)
    Not since 1962
    Seldom updated
    About every three years
    Five to six years
    Not for several years
    Just received new text this semester
    I don't know
    Not often for textbook, but the reading lists and manuals are under
       constant revision.
    10 No answers

career counseling had received none at their schools.[6] More than
seven out of ten respondents say that they get such guidance
outside the school setting, primarily from their parents. This is a
source which is either unavailable or of little use to the young men
of Watts and east Los Angeles, because those who might provide
this assistance are absent or are themselves unemployed or underemployed.

"When I was in school, it was more common for a student to
take what the teacher said verbatim—it's almost like the word of

God. They go strictly by that. And then when you get out there and all the stuff is different, you know you're lost. Nine times out of ten when you graduate you going to your parents and you can't really get help there. And maybe family pull will get you a job similar to what your father had, something like that. And then they're not even satisfied with that because they know you can do better than that. And that's something that your father's been doing, not that he is particularly proud of it; and what might happen, you might do the same thing your father did, not because your father decided to do it but because he knew somebody—like his boss or somebody—had enough pity, you know, to hire you" (Alfred Jackson).

To the extent that youngsters in the ghetto and barrio get information and counseling (or even education) at all, it is ironic that often they will get it from one another and not from the household, the school system, or the public agencies. After all, the street youngster spends much of his time "rapping" with his partners. In the process he develops an articulateness which is rarely recognized and used productively by the schools, and also receives and conveys whatever facts or ideas may be available at the time. This informal network of communication, indoctrination, and education is the means by which most street youngsters raise themselves to maturity, for better or for worse. As one east Los Angeles youngster has already commented, he learned much more from his associates on the street than he ever did in school. A bright and verbal Watts youngster discussed the same phenomenon, in the context of his own household and his impression of his younger brother and friends:

"I think it really amounts to rebellion, in a good sense, because their rebellion is not a destructive kind. It's the kind that, if it's possible, I think they would rather spend three hours in a classroom talking to a teacher that maybe made a mistake, and maybe get that teacher to admit to that mistake, admit that he was wrong. And, see, most of the time that the teacher was wrong, when I was there you just accepted it. They don't accept it now. And he [my brother] is more aware. Like a whole lot of times he couldn't wait to go to school because the teacher said something the day before and he might have come home and looked in the encyclopedia and found out that she was wrong or he was wrong. Sometimes they come home with eight or nine kids where they walk to the house arguing about what the teacher said. I think him and his close friends—they're all like that. They'll come home and argue about a hypothetical problem that isn't really relevant to what they're doing, but they have just enough interest and want to know something" (Alfred Jackson).

"Interest" is a key word here, because the ghetto youngster has a low tolerance for boredom and pure routine. His demands undoubtedly are unreasonable at times: much of what we must do in the process of acquiring knowledge and performing work is inherently or inescapably uninteresting. Yet there is also a great deal more that society could do to engage the interests and motivation of the young in both the educational and work processes.

Students' criticisms of Los Angeles schools stem from a conviction that most schools make little or no attempt to educate the mass of students and concentrate, at best, upon the "college preparatory" and, particularly, the "good" students among them who are favored by teachers and administrators. Hence for many youngsters their attendance at school is really unrelated to the question of whether they receive a quality education, unless they happen to fall in the favored category: "I mean the first reason why they drop out, because in school they're in dumps, nothing to relate to; they give you the classes that they want to give you, you know, like they put you in college prep, or general business and all that. They say you take this 'cause it's going to be better for you later in life, and then they give it to the other people who have better grades than you. They just put you on a level, they categorize you on a level of pure grades. They don't grade you on your education, they grade you on how often you come to school. If you come to school every day and don't do nothing, they'll pass you along. If you come to school, you'll pass, you know. Hell, what's the use of staying in? I graduated for my mother, man, 'cause it made my mother more happy, you know, not that I'm a momma's boy; I didn't learn shit" (Earl).

Some of the youngsters feel that this handicaps them in the future because they have not received a meaningful education and because a massive lack of interest on the part of counselors prevents them from getting the help and information they need. Most specifically, the alleged failure of schools to offer a good education, counseling, and preparation for work means that the young man is at a disadvantage when he first applies for a suitable job. He may or may not have a diploma, as arbitrarily required by many employers, but even if he has the "credentials" in this respect, standard tests may still disqualify him: "Okay, before I found out about this job I went down to the post office in my community and the man told me that I was a week late 'cause I could have got a job there as a postal clerk or something, you know, because you have to take a test to see if you qualify. Like why don't they tell you—like sending out letters or something like that to let you know? Well, 'cause a lot of time jobs are open, it's just that people don't know about them" (Robert).

Feelings of this sort are common: "On the testing thing, they might give you a test, you know, to a Black person that for even high school students might be difficult to pass. If you don't pass that test, you don't get no job. See, they base the person on if they pass the test or not, but not on how good the individual works on the job, or would he be essential to the job—that test thing, if you don't pass the test, you don't get no job. So you can't really base a person on how he did on the test because he might come up on the job which he *will* need, most likely. Most Black people will need a job based on that" (George—south Los Angeles).

"Like, I was in this student training program, you know. I've been in it for a year—I'm still on it. Afterwards they're supposed to promote you to a messenger clerk and you take a test, you know, but that test isn't relevant, you know, 'cause they come out with things they ask—I don't know, weird things—math and things you never learn in school because the schools are messed up. . . . They give you about three questions about the job you're doing and that's all" (Earl).

It is interesting that many of the young people will distinguish among schools and among students in assessing the relative responsibilities for such deficiencies. In south Los Angeles, for example, Locke is regarded generally as a better high school than Jordan, but some of the youngsters think that this is as much the result of student motivation as it is of superior teaching. They tend to feel that the most effective education occurs when there is just the right match among students, class and teacher, and that counselors are very often responsible for the failure to make this match. They complain of too little individual attention, and at some schools the unmotivated students will make it difficult for the more motivated to learn anything. Many of them are aware of the complexities inherent in this problem, but do not regard this fact as sufficient to exculpate the schools from their considerable share of the blame.

It is almost a cliché that the route to success and escape from the ghetto lies in education and training. Much of the existing antipoverty effort rests upon this premise, and many younger residents share this same belief. Particularly in Watts the young men tend to associate their chances for career attainment with their educational prospects, and pessimism is often related to a perception that their existing schooling is inadequate and that they may never have an opportunity to fill the gap. They suspect that their education has little or no substance in it, and largely because they *do* associate prospects for success with a good education, they can become even more deeply pessimistic as they enter the labor market.

NOTES

1. Our survey results and observations correspond perfectly with the findings of Dr. Marvin L. Marshall, whose USC doctoral dissertation reported in 1968 that less than one third of recent graduates in nine Los Angeles high schools could remember tenth grade guidance as such.

2. Three quarters of the counselors and guidance teachers who answered my question reported that the test results and other information from guidance are used in counseling only "occasionally" or "rarely".

3. According to the estimates of our interviewers and interviewees, about three tenths of Locke pupils come from households receiving incomes of $6000 a year or more, compared to only 10 percent of those at Jordan. Almost 27 percent of the Jordan pupils live in households getting less than $4000 a year, compared to about 15 percent at Locke.

4. The students at James Garfield High School in east Los Angeles showed more contact than others. There may be a special reason for this. For three years a specialized counseling program—the Garfield Educational Complex Center—has served Garfield students and attempted to assist potential dropouts who needed economic support in order to remain in school. According to data provided by a staff member of the Center, the Center has been able to find part-time employment or summer work for high percentages of those who apply for it. Since our own survey findings show that youngsters in low-income areas must often rely on the school to find or develop employment for them, obviously the Garfield program has been of some importance, and our figures suggest that it has markedly increased the contact between students and vocational counselors or work coordinators.

5. Whatever progress has been made in this area, since I first studied the question in 1963, appears to be mainly semantic. What is now termed the

"opportunity transfer" was then called the "social adjustment transfer." What was then called the "dropout rate" is now labeled "attrition."

6. *Guidance Practices Leading to Career Orientation and Instruction for Selected Secondary School Students of Connecticut*, Department of Higher, Technical, and Adult Education, University of Connecticut, January 1970, pp. 36-37.

# 4

---

# ENTERING THE LABOR MARKET

When he first enters the labor market, the young man from Watts or east Los Angeles is very much "on his own." There is probably more parental guidance in the Chicano than in the Black Community, but both groups seek and find employment primarily through informal and personal channels. A great many young men will make their earliest contact with the "labor market" through what we have termed the subeconomy, a subject which is a major focus of later chapters of this book. Some get their jobs through the school, the Employment Service, or a federally funded program such as a Teen Post, but most report that they find work with the help of friends and relatives or strictly on their own. This job-seeking pattern is consistent and pervasive in both communities, with one interesting variation: the Black youngsters receive relatively more help from governmental, organizational, or school sources, while the Chicano youngsters rely proportionately more upon direct applications to employers. Once having entered the labor market the Chicanos penetrate the clerical, semiskilled and skilled categories to a greater degree than do the Blacks, but teenagers in both areas are concentrated in service, unskilled, and "other" occupations.

One generalization is immediately possible: the public employment services and funded training programs (including, of course, the highly touted NAB-JOBS program for subsidized on-the-job training by private employers) are largely irrelevant, from the perspective of Black and Chicano young men in communities like Watts and east Los Angeles. The overwhelming majority find their employment, if any, without the visible assistance of the Employment Service, and almost none obtain permanent employment which has a demonstrable relationship to participation in available training. Indeed, the majority show little or no awareness of the training programs in or near their respective communities. This result is especially striking in Watts, where a number of training centers are located.

## Jobseeking in the Ghetto and Barrio

In south Los Angeles almost half of those holding a job, at the time of survey, had found it through friends and relatives or by direct application to the employer. Another 17 percent had been aided by a school; about equal percentages (5 percent, respectively) had used want ads or private employment agencies; and another 6 percent had used unidentified "other" sources. Only about one in five had been steered into their work by the Employment Service.

In east Los Angeles almost seven of ten young workers had obtained their present work through friends and relatives or by direct application to the employer. About one in ten had found it through a school; only 3.2 percent and 2.4 percent, respectively, had used want ads or private employment agencies; and almost one in ten had made use of unidentified "other" sources. Only 6.5 percent had been assisted by the Employment Service.

In total, a little over one third of the Blacks in our sample had found their present work through the school or the Employment Service—much above the 17.6 percent figure for the Chicanos. Chicanos, on the other hand, had made proportionately greater use of the "walk-in" (direct application) technique: almost 25 percent had used this channel in contrast with less than 13 percent of the

Blacks. Correspondingly, about 43 percent of the Chicanos had been guided by friends and relatives, compared to a third of the Blacks. Thus the Blacks got significantly more help from public or federally funded institutions, while the Chicanos relied overwhelmingly on their own personal or internal resources. In neither case, however, were existing public agencies the major source of assistance.

For Blacks in particular, the "other" category appears to reflect assistance from organizations like a Teen Post (a federally funded recreational and cultural program for teenagers), the Watts Labor Community Action Committee (WLCAC), and so forth. The corresponding category in east Los Angeles is more difficult to evaluate, but it does not appear that the Chicanos received the same volume of support from the types of organizations mentioned above. It is difficult to know the extent to which this may reflect the fact that young Chicanos may not need such help so intensely, or the possibility that there are cultural, administrative, or political influences at work.

## Table 5.

### *Job-seeking Methods (Percent)*

| | | Men ages 16-19 | | | |
|---|---|---|---|---|---|
| | 6 UES Poverty Areas Total 1968-69* | L.A. UES Areas 1968-69* | | IIR Survey 1971 (*Most recent or previous job*) | |
| Employment Service | 15.5 | 18.2 | 14.6 | 9.5 | 3.4 |
| Employer | 25.1 | 27.3 | 24.4 | 20.0 | 18.6 |
| Relatives, etc. | 21.3 | 27.3 | 24.4 | 50.5 | 23.7 |
| Newspapers | 18.5 | 13.6 | 12.2 | 1.1 | |
| School | | | | 14.7 | 28.8 |
| Private Agency | 4.8 | | 2.4 | | 3.4 |
| Organization | 7.9 | 9.1 | 17.1 | | |
| Union | | | 2.4 | 4.2 | 22.0 |
| Pickup Location | | | | | |
| Other | 7.0 | 4.5 | 2.4 | | |

\* Methods used during previous 12-month period.

The experience of teenagers in the two areas especially emphasizes the informality of the job-hunting process. Almost three quarters of the east Los Angeles teenagers had found their jobs through friends and relatives or direct application. About 13 percent had been aided by the school, and barely over 4 percent had used the Employment Service in finding their work. About 37 percent of the Watts teenagers had been aided by friends or relatives, but a smaller percentage had used the "walk-in" method than those in east Los Angeles and much larger percentages had used the school (26.7 percent) and the Employment Service (10 percent). In both areas the young *adults* reported proportionately more use of the Employment Service in finding their present work (9.6 percent in east Los Angeles and 24.6 percent in south Los Angeles). In south Los Angeles the adults had used the direct application method much more than had the teenagers.

The above figures, of course, apply to those who were employed at the time of our survey. Among all those (employed, unemployed, or in school) who reported on their previous employment, the pattern is much the same. The teenagers rely heavily upon friends and relatives or "walk-in" in east Los Angeles, whereas the south Los Angeles youngsters depend more upon the school and "other" sources and relatively less (though still considerably) upon the standard informal sources. No age group had been assisted significantly by the Employment Service.

Among only the currently *un*employed, the south Los Angeles group again relies overwhelmingly upon friends and relatives, direct application, and "other" sources, in that order. By contrast, those currently employed indicate proportionately greater assistance from the Employment Service and the school and relatively less upon "walk-in" and "other." The unemployed in east Los Angeles report some past help from the Employment Service, but slightly over two thirds had secured employment through friends and relatives (preeminently) or direct application. The employed in that area had used those two methods *even more,* though with somewhat greater reliance on direct application and proportionately less on friends and relatives.

When job-finding techniques are examined by the type of work presently and/or formerly performed by the person surveyed, we find that the pattern described previously is fairly consistent for all types of employment. Among the presently employed, both the Chicanos and Blacks had secured all types of work primarily through friends and relatives or direct application, although the Chicanos consistently had been relatively more successful with the "walk-in" method than had the Blacks. In south Los Angeles the small number of semiskilled and professional workers showed the highest percentage use of the Employment Service; in east Los Angeles, the percentage pattern is mixed, but only 8 workers out of 119 credited their employment to the Employment Service.

A tentative generalization, based on the current and most recent work, is that both Chicanos and Blacks predominantly get their jobs through informal and private channels, with some use of the Employment Service at low job levels in east Los Angeles and higher levels in south Los Angeles. In both areas, of course, those youngsters who hold or have held school-related jobs had obtained them through the school itself. Asked about the type of jobs that they can get through the school, the youngsters' answers often reflected disdain and skepticism: "That's only about eight hours a week. Keep your mind lowered, you know, just keep sweeping a broom, 'you might even be head custodian' " (Alex).

In south Los Angeles there appears to be somewhat more successful usage of the Employment Service among high school graduates than among dropouts, while in east Los Angeles the pattern seems to be reversed. Dropouts in both areas have less success with the "walk-in" method, and rely proportionately more upon friends and relatives or "other" sources. Youngsters in households headed by the mother find relatively fewer jobs through their friends and relatives, and apparently rely somewhat more upon the school, the Employment Service, and "other" sources.

Consistent with the employment patterns described previously, east Los Angeles respondents in the higher-paid ($3.00 an hour or more) jobs had found them overwhelmingly through informal channels; those in south Los Angeles also had relied heavily on those same sources, but successful usage of the Employment Service was reported by nearly 30 percent of those whose previous job had paid at least $3.00 per hour.

There is some evidence that the amount of contact with the Department of Human Resources Development (HRD) is positively related to labor market information; those who did relatively poorly on our information quiz (four job definitions and four evaluations of relative pay for specified jobs) generally indicated less contact with HRD. However, on the question (the definition of "machinist") which seemed to be the most valid indicator of degree of information, there is no significant difference between the "contact" and "no contact" groups, and it would seem that knowledge, in this case, is related most directly to actual labor market experience. This area will be explored in Chapter 5.

While, in general, there is little relationship between one's major in high school and the other variables, there is evidence in our survey that college preparatory majors obtain a higher proportion of the school-related jobs than do the vocational or industrial arts majors. This may be some confirmation of the statement made by teenage interviewees that school administrators show favoritism in the allocation of and referrals to employment, and would tend to favor the "better" students (more of whom, presumably, would be college prep majors).

By and large, the jobseeking methods used predominantly in poverty areas seem to correspond with those generally used in nonpoverty areas, with some variations.[1] Nonpoverty job-seekers appear to rely somewhat more upon direct applications to employers and want ads, while poverty residents make proportionately greater use of the Employment Service and community organizations. In general, the differences are small, and it might be concluded that minority youngsters suffer no special disadvantage from their reliance upon informal job-seeking channels. This conclusion would be incorrect. Those with parents and friends already located in permanent jobs have a marked advantage over those without parent or friends who are similarly situated in the labor market.

## Patterns of Employment

Most of the teenagers in Watts and east Los Angeles obviously enter the labor market at low levels and, with some exceptions, tend to stay there. Even the young adults are very often to be found in those categories, though Chicanos succeed in getting semiskilled, skilled and clerical jobs in somewhat higher proportions than do Blacks. Watts teenagers are located in school, governmental and organizational jobs to a much greater degree than Chicano youngsters, and Chicano teenagers are proportionately more concentrated in service, clerical and "other" categories. Altogether, slightly over half of the employed Chicano teenagers surveyed are in service and unskilled categories, compared to about 43 percent of the Blacks. Almost a quarter of the south Los Angeles teenagers are in employment connected with a school, and about 10 percent are in government work of some kind (post office, etc.). Nearly 5 percent have organizational jobs.

In south Los Angeles the age 20-24 group among the employed is located in service work in almost the same proportion as the teenagers, but otherwise it reflects a higher concentration in semiskilled, professional and skilled jobs and much less in the unskilled category. In east Los Angeles, the pattern by age group also changes, but in different directions. The young adults are much less concentrated than are the teenagers in service occupations, and are more frequently to be found in clerical, semiskilled and skilled jobs. In total, almost two thirds of the Chicano 20-24 group are in clerical, semiskilled, skilled and professional jobs, compared to about 38 percent of the Blacks.[2] The older group in east Los Angeles had been more successful in moving out of the lowest job classifications than had the same group in Watts, but again it must be remembered that the Chicanos in our survey come from proportionately more households receiving $6000 a year and over. With this fact in mind, it is then worthy of note that only a total of 22 percent of the Chicano young adults are located in the skilled blue-collar and professional white-collar occupations. This is only slightly better than the corresponding labor market pattern in south Los Angeles, where about 17 percent of the young adults are in those same jobs. The difference between the two areas lies in the greater penetration of Chicanos into the clerical, sales, and semiskilled jobs. Except for certain semiskilled occupations, those jobs often pay less than the service, governmental and school jobs in which the Blacks remain heavily concentrated.

When we move to the total sample (employed, unemployed, in-school, etc.) and examine the patterns of previous employment and pay levels, there are interesting variations in both areas and age groups. The past employment of Chicanos, in both the teenage and young adult categories, reflects a higher concentration in semiskilled jobs than is true of the presently employed. Currently employed Black and Chicano teenagers show a much higher concentration in school-related jobs than in the past, but this is particularly significant and striking in the case of the Blacks.

Proportions of employment in service occupations remain consistently high for both areas and age groups. The proportions in government work have increased for the Blacks and diminished for the Browns. On the other hand, the percentage of Black teenagers in unskilled work has appeared to increase while the corresponding proportion of Chicano teenagers has decreased slightly.

An analysis of the three most recent jobs held (prior to the current employment of those employed at survey time) by all those surveyed reveals little consistent evidence of improvement in pay and status as the respondents moved from one job to another. The pattern, in fact, is considerably mixed. For Black teenagers, the employment situation seemed to worsen over time, with about 54 percent concentrated in the below-$1.75 category during the most recent period of work in contrast with somewhat more than four tenths in prior periods. Black young adults increased their percentages at both ends of the pay ladder, increasing their proportion slightly in the lowest pay categories and significantly in the $3.00-plus bracket.

In like manner, the Chicano young adults sharply boosted their percentage in the $3.00-plus category over time, but in contrast to the Blacks, also cut their percentage representation in the lowest categories. The Chicano teenagers cut their percentage in the below-$1.75 category slightly and increased their representation in the $2.00 to $2.49 bracket as they progressed from job to job. Thus for our sample there are indications that Chicanos improve their labor market position to some degree as they move from earlier to more recent jobs. Among Chicano teenagers, however, well over half earn *under* $2.00 per hour, and this high percentage has persisted through their work experience. Even among the Chicano adults in our survey, approximately two tenths to one quarter have remained in that low category of pay as they shifted from job 3 to job 1 (in our numbering the most recent job).

The relationship between vocational training and the labor market experience is perhaps more mystifying and shocking than any other aspect of this study. The percentage of *unemployment* is consistently as high among those reporting special job training than it is among those reporting none. When we examine the relationship between educational attainment and labor market status, the pattern is somewhat mixed. In south Los Angeles, proportionately more high school *graduates* than dropouts are unemployed; in east Los Angeles, the graduates do proportionately better, but the difference is not wide. In analyzing the pay rates reported for successive jobs, we find that in south Los Angeles those *without* training do about as well as or better than those *with* training in penetrating the higher pay levels or avoiding the lower; in east Los Angeles the percentage of the defined group in the $3.00-plus category is consistently higher for those *without* training, and usually a smaller percentage of the "no training" group is in the below-$1.75 bracket.

In both areas the graduates generally do better than dropouts in attaining the higher pay level—a result more in line with what we would normally expect. In the most recent job, however, about one quarter of the graduates in both areas were in the below-$1.75 category. Every bit of evidence emerging from our survey confirms that economic trends over the past few years have had a particularly deleterious effect upon the labor market position of young men in central city ghettos and barrios.

The unusual and startling nature of certain of these results leads naturally to some wide-ranging speculations about their possible significance. One clue is the quantitative importance of the "other" category in most of the relationships we have examined. This omnibus grouping includes a great many young persons in east and south Los Angeles who, apparently, have left the labor market or never entered it. It is both ironic and understandable that those who have had training would be strongly resistant to accepting work at a lower level than that for which, theoretically, they have been trained. The "reservation price" for their labor, in economic terms, will rise in accordance with their expectations, and some will probably prefer to remain (technically) unemployed rather than accept the low-status, low-paid employment which is offered.

"If they start a program I'll shine it on [ignore it] because they are going to give you the same old thing. Like when I go for a job I'll go on my own, but yet in school they don't let me know where the jobs are available; it could benefit me, you know, 'cause the jobs that I get are chicken shit, rinky dink things, you know. And then when you go for a job the people check you out and see how you are; if they don't like the way you look, they'll harass you, like that's what's been happening to me a lot. They've just been giving me hours that don't really mean nothing, but they wanted me to work the way they wanted me to work, you know. And it just doesn't help you out, man. This is a little bit money in your pocket, but then again it ain't worth it" (Earl—east Los Angeles).

"Over there in the factory, when he [a vocational teacher] took us over there, they let us go over everything real good, and we saw that they were doing the same basic thing that we were doing at school, except it was on a more complex level. When we got back to the school that evening, he told us that all of us qualified, you know. As far as working, there wouldn't be no problem in getting a job; a letter from him would do it. But there were six of us then, only three went down there. I wasn't one of them. He had talked to us and told us that it would be better to try something else. Just in that factory alone, there were about three guys killed last year. And another thing, when we walked through there, especially the Negro guy, he'd say, 'You don't want to work here', stuff like that. Especially during the lunch break, we was standing out front and so I walked back into the main part, and I was standing behind the yellow line so I could watch them. One guy came over and told me, he said, 'Listen, if you can do anything better than this, go ahead and get it'. What he said, he was doing it because it was the only means of immediate support for him and his family" (Alfred Jackson).

"For $1.65 I wouldn't mind sitting back on my ass, working at a bank or something, but you carry a rake and get a dollar and a quarter an hour, that's really hard labor, man. I figure a cat should get paid at least $3.00 and up, you know, for getting out there breaking his back in the sun, man. They don't want to pay no money. And then they got brothers and sisters walking up and down the streets sweating for an hour—they stand there in the same line every day for $1.65, doing the same kind of work. I can see this only to the sense where all of these cats coming in, going out in junior high school just working for their little $1.65—I can see that's pretty good for junior high school students, but when you get to high school and start getting up into the higher stage of life, you know, you gonna need some money, man. You can't be working for no penny-pinch. That's not my stick, you know. I'm educated, man" (Gregory—south Los Angeles).

It is an observable fact that jobs are scarce even for the graduates of existing training programs, and that many programs are regarded by trainer and trainee alike as a source of immediate income rather than as a preparation for long-term careers at a level above the average in the ghetto or barrio. The past failure of the economy to absorb some training program graduates into permanent employment, now exacerbated by a major recession, feeds the cynicism of those already inclined to be cynical. Some may be motivated to remain in the subeconomy, or perhaps another part of that shadowy territory which is on the margin of what we call the labor market.

## The Unemployed

When we construct a profile of the currently unemployed and compare it with that of the employed, some interesting similarities and differences come to light. For instance, both the employed and unemployed are generally concentrated in the lower skill categories, but in both south and east Los Angeles the semiskilled workers are represented markedly more among the unemployed than among the employed. Proportionately more of the employed are in the clerical and governmental categories. All of our figures

**Table 6.**

*Selected Comparisons of the Employed and Unemployed, by Area (Percent)*

|  |  | Employed | | Unemployed | |
|---|---|---|---|---|---|
|  |  | South LA | East LA | South LA | East LA |
| Whether | Trained |  |  |  |  |
|  | Yes | 20.8 | 9.7 | 25.6 | 13.9 |
|  | No | 79.2 | 90.3 | 74.4 | 86.1 |
| Highest Grade Completed |  |  |  |  |  |
|  | 9th | 0.0 | 0.0 | 5.4 | 0.0 |
|  | 10th | 15.0 | 10.6 | 5.4 | 14.3 |
|  | 11th | 10.0 | 19.1 | 27.0 | 28.6 |
|  | 12th | 52.5 | 46.8 | 43.2 | 52.9 |
|  | Other | 22.5 | 23.5 | 19.0 | 14.2 |
| Head of Household |  |  |  |  |  |
|  | Person | 72.7 | 29.2 | 52.0 | 19.0 |
|  | Father | 9.1 | 50.0 | 22.0 | 50.0 |
|  | Mother | 14.5 | 16.0 | 26.0 | 19.0 |
|  | Other | 3.6 | 4.7 | 0.0 | 12.0 |

suggest that high proportions of those whose past employment has been semiskilled have suffered unemployment during the ongoing recession.

The amount of reported training does not distinguish the employed from the unemployed. Indeed, higher percentages among the *unemployed* report special training. This, of course, is simply another reflection of the market phenomenon discussed earlier.

Dropouts are represented in higher relative numbers among the unemployed, though the majority of unemployed youngsters in both areas have high school diplomas. Among the unemployed, about 57 percent in east Los Angeles and 62 percent in south Los Angeles are high school graduates, of whom many have had some college work. By contrast, three quarters of the employed in south Los Angeles and seven tenths in east Los Angeles had at least graduated from high school.

In south Los Angeles the burden of unemployment is heavier for the young man than it is in the east Los Angeles area, because a much greater proportion of the unemployed may be found in households headed by someone other than the father. More than half of the unemployed youngsters in Watts are themselves the head of household, compared to less than a fifth of the Chicanos. Over 80 percent of the Black unemployed and half of the Chicano live in households headed by themselves, their mother, or a nonparental relative or friend. As pointed out before, high levels of youth unemployment and underemployment can have disastrous social and economic consequences in those communities characterized by family disorganization. Although this problem may not be as serious in east as in south Los Angeles, it must be noted that it still affects a high percentage of the Chicano households and that many of the households, even among those headed by the male parent, continue to fall in lower income brackets. In our east Los Angeles sample, which appears to be better off economically than the average for that community, more than four tenths of the households receive under $6000 in annual income.

All of these findings demonstrate the continued severity of unemployment in the areas surveyed and the relative inefficacy of established training and employment programs. The argument has sometimes been made, in response to such findings, that the beneficial effects of those programs are not reflected in surveys of low-income ghettos, because those who benefit will tend to move out of the community. Nothing in our study can either prove or disprove that theory, and to my knowledge no other survey has yet provided an answer. Our survey *does* show that significant percentages of young men in those communities have obtained both academic and vocational training without measurable benefit to themselves in the labor market.

It will be argued, of course, that their failure to benefit does not result from deficiencies or limitations in education and training, but rather from employer policies which discriminate against young men because of race or national origin, police records, cultural differences, rigid credential or degree requirements, and so forth. It could be added that the unfavorable labor market experience suffered by these youngsters is also the consequence of general economic decline. Much or all of this may be true, but it merely serves to corroborate a major point of this study: that too much attention has been paid to the supply side of the youth labor market and not enough to the demand. The importance of this will be discussed and demonstrated in later chapters.

## NOTES

1. For a summary of these findings, see Harvey J. Hilaski, "How Poverty Area Residents Look for Work," *Monthly Labor Review*, March 1971, pp. 41-45.

2. One major problem emphasized by our analysis of the ghetto labor market is that the prevailing definitions of employment categories (service, semiskilled, professional, etc.) are highly deficient for analytical purposes. In categorizing jobs we used the official Census Bureau manual, but logically it makes little sense, e.g. to lump together policemen and janitors in one occupational category, and the distinctions between the service and unskilled categories are blurred at best.

# 5

## LABOR MARKET INFORMATION AND PERCEPTIONS

Young men in Watts and east Los Angeles begin their employment with little guidance and a highly restricted and unbalanced view of future possibilities. The burden, we found, is heavier on the Blacks than on the Chicanos, but neither group is substantially assisted by the educational system or by public agencies in the quest for knowledge or for work.

There are some qualifications to this dim and pessimistic appraisal. With a couple of exceptions, the majority of the young men surveyed did reasonably well in our short quiz about jobs, and the Chicanos, in particular, appear to glean a reasonable amount of practical information from their higher participation in the labor market and their penetration of a somewhat greater variety of jobs.

In order to test the degree of labor market information in a way which will make it possible to compare our results with those obtained in other studies, we used eight questions which had been asked earlier in the nationwide longitudinal study conducted (and still in progress) by Professor Herbert S. Parnes and his associates at The Ohio State University, previously referred to.[1] We were unable to replicate the entire Parnes study of job knowledge, but we selected four questions concerning job content and four concerning relative pay rates, covering occupations at varying levels of skills. Respondents were asked to define "hospital orderly," "machinist," "draftsman," and "social worker," by checking the appropriate multiple choice answer, and to indicate which one of the following pairs of occupations pays more on the average: (1) auto mechanic or electrician; (2) truck driver or grocery store clerk; (3) lawyer or high school teacher; and (4) janitor or policeman.

The interviewees were also asked whether they knew anything about certain training programs in their respective communities. Each of our survey interviewers carried a mimeographed list of *all* major programs, complete with phone numbers, addresses and brief descriptions, and were instructed to read off the titles of the training agencies or hand the list to the respondent for his perusal. After the relevant question had been asked, the respondent could keep the list for his further guidance and information. Very few in either area expressed an interest in retaining the list.

As a test of perceptions, the young men were asked to estimate how much an average American family makes during a year, and how much they thought it *should* make. We did not intend this as an information quiz, because relatively few Americans know the precise average family income, but rather as an indication of the respondent's subjective evaluation. He was also asked to state his preference, for the *near* or *immediate* future, among the following alternatives: (1) finish high school and go straight into full-time work (if he has not finished high school); (2) finish college and then go into full-time work (if he has not finished college); (3) enter a special training program and then get full-time work; (4) go directly into full-time work as soon as possible, getting whatever training is needed on the job (if not already in full-time work; (5) go into regular work but have some time off with pay or reimbursement during the day to go to school; or (6) go into regular work and go to school at night (on his own time).

One purpose of this question was to test the potential response to new combinations of work and education, as reflected partly in alternative #5 above and suggested as a desirable possibility by such manpower experts as Assistant Secretary of Labor Jerome Rosow.[2] Unfortunately, its inclusion in a list of alternatives toward the end of a long interview probably caused many respondents to overlook it. In addition, it is an unfamiliar concept and perhaps the first tendency of a respondent is to choose an alternative which seems more familiar and more feasible. Nevertheless, a noticeable percentage of interviews did express an interest.

Of the questions asked (taken from the Parnes survey), three in particular—the definition of "machinist" and "hospital orderly" and the relative pay for "auto mechanic or electrician"—appeared to be of greatest difficulty for the respondents in our samples. It is interesting that, as a general rule, the interviewees seem to know much more about relative pay rates than about job definitions. Their "income consciousness" is such that they are likely to know whether one job pays more than another even when they may have some difficulty in defining the respective jobs.

The results obtained from our survey of labor market information and perceptions should be reviewed in the light of certain fundamental differences between the east Los Angeles and Watts samples:

(1) Relatively more of the Chicanos interviewed reside in households earning $6000 a year and over;

(2) Proportionately, many more of the Blacks live in households headed by their mother or themselves;

(3) The Chicanos have a higher labor force participation rate than the Blacks in our survey;

(4) In the labor market, Chicanos are somewhat more successful than Blacks in securing semiskilled and skilled work, though youngsters in both groups are generally concentrated in the lower-skill categories;

(5) Many of the Chicano teenagers attend schools outside the Los Angeles City School District, some of which offer no guidance courses or vocational counseling, while almost all of the Black teenagers attend District schools;

(6) The majority of the Watts teenagers still in school attend either Jordan or Locke High Schools, and the previously described differences between those two schools should be kept in mind; and

(7) The Watts community geographically is much smaller than east Los Angeles, and one Skills Center and several other training or employment programs are located in Watts itself, thereby making the potential awareness of such facilities seemingly greater

there than it should be in the vastly larger east Los Angeles community.

## Information and Knowledge

Certain generalizations quickly become apparent as the results of the surveys in south and east Los Angeles are sifted and analyzed:

(1) The Chicanos consistently tend to score higher on the information quiz than do the Blacks in our samples.

(2) This tendency is probably related to degree of labor force participation and experience reported by the groups. Other tests also show that there is a positive correlation between extent of employment and knowledge of jobs; for instance, the currently employed tend to have more information than do the currently unemployed or the students.

(3) In south Los Angeles, those in the lowest and highest income households usually do significantly better on the quiz than those in the middle, while in east Los Angeles there is a more mixed pattern.

(4) In general, relatively greater knowledge is displayed by those who say that they have had job referrals from friends and relatives or the Department of Human Resources Development (HRD), as compared to those who say that they have never received assistance from those sources.

(5) Those who report that they were (or are) college preparatory majors in high school usually score higher than do those who major in vocational or industrial arts programs.

(6) While high school graduates (and, in greater degree, those who have had at least some college) usually do better than the dropouts, the differences often are small and the relationship is neither as strong nor as consistent as it is in the cases noted above.

(7) In like manner, those who recall taking the guidance class and an aptitude test usually do somewhat better, but the relationship does not appear to be significant for a number of reasons.

(8) In general, those who report participation in a training program do no better on the quiz than do those who are untrained. Similarly, there is little observable relationship between the *nature* of present or previous employment and labor market knowledge, although our samples in the higher job categories

## Table 7.
### *Labor Market Awareness:*
### *Knowledge of Jobs, by Age and Area*
### *(Percent Giving Correct Definition)*

| Job Defined | East Los Angeles | | South Los Angeles | |
|---|---|---|---|---|
| | 16-19 | 20-24 | 16-19 | 20-24 |
| Hospital Orderly | 52.1 | 60.0 | 51.2 | 53.4 |
| Machinist | 58.6 | 73.8 | 33.3 | 52.9 |
| Draftsman | 85.2 | 92.9 | 63.1 | 89.0 |
| Social Worker | 82.4 | 89.4 | 62.8 | 85.2 |

*Knowledge of Relative Job Earnings, by Age and Area*
*(Percent Giving Correct Answer)*

| (Question: Who earns more in a year?) | | | | |
|---|---|---|---|---|
| (1) Auto Mechanic or Electrician | 80.6 | 84.9 | 68.5 | 78.9 |
| (2) Truck Driver or Grocery Clerk | 88.9 | 91.8 | 80.9 | 87.5 |
| (3) Lawyer or High School Teacher | 95.2 | 95.4 | 88.0 | 87.5 |
| (4) Janitor or Policeman | 83.4 | 89.5 | 81.5 | 87.4 |

*Awareness of Training by Age and Area (Percent)*

| | | | | |
|---|---|---|---|---|
| Yes | 32.6 | 31.9 | 25.0 | 50.0 |
| No | 67.4 | 68.1 | 75.0 | 50.0 |

(skilled labor, professional and technical, etc.) are usually so small that definite conclusions are risky or impossible.

Perhaps the strongest generalization which emerges from this study is that there is a close relationship between labor market participation and knowledge. One problem, inevitably, is to separate cause from effect in this kind of relationship: correlations only suggest that two variables are associated in some reasonably predictable way, but cannot demonstrate whether one or the other of the variables is causal or whether both are responding simultaneously to a third variable. In our case does a young man in east Los Angeles or Watts participate more often in the market because he has greater knowledge and information or does he know more because he has participated to a greater degree? Or are both knowledge and participation related to entirely independent variables?

A process of elimination may help us to isolate the variables which are most likely to have a causal role. The potential sources of labor market information and guidance are: (1) the household, and especially the father or other male adult who has had labor market experience; 2) friends and acquaintances; 3) the school; 4) public agencies or community organizations; and 5) the labor market itself. Statistically, we already know that about seven tenths of the total south Los Angeles sample and about 45 percent of the total east Los Angeles sample are in households headed by themselves or someone other than the male parent, and in addition we discovered in the survey that there is no predictable relationship between job knowledge and whether or not the respondent had *ever* discussed jobs with his father. We know also that in south Los Angeles most of the teenagers are in households headed by someone other than their father.

We know that in both areas job-seeking is performed predominantly in private and informal ways, with heavy reliance upon friends and relatives or direct application to employers. In neither area is the guidance class or counseling in school perceived as being helpful as a source of useful information. The Chicanos in our sample, who evinced a greater amount of knowledge in the quiz, had markedly less contact with public agencies (such as HRD) and community organizations. On the other hand, they participate to a higher degree in the labor market, experience less unemployment, and show higher percentages of penetration into production and clerical work.

It would appear, therefore, that in both communities labor market knowledge is most likely to be the *result* of exposure to jobs in the market and informal counseling and referrals by friends and relatives. The parental role is undoubtedly stronger in east Los Angeles than in Watts: a much higher proportion of the Chicanos, for example, report that they have at least discussed jobs with their fathers. In neither case does it seem likely that the school, public agencies, or other informational sources have had an important impact.

It is clear that the effect of labor market participation is circular. As the individual gains exposure to jobs as the consequence of informal guidance from his father and his friends, he in turn passes along his knowledge to his own children and friends. Once the members of a given group have successfully entered the labor market, that fact strengthens the potential for success among others in their group. On the other hand, a series of unsuccessful or unproductive experiences in the market will increase the probability of additional failures in that group, because the channels of useful guidance and information are thereby more limited and less available.

The importance of personal observation and experience in influencing the degree and accuracy of labor market information can be illustrated in a number of concrete ways. One revealing illustration emerges from our analysis of relative degrees of information held by students at Jordan and Locke High Schools in the Watts area, where academically and economically the Locke students are regarded as more advantaged. Of the eight knowledge questions in the quiz, Locke students did proportionately better on five of them. Jordan students did somewhat better than Locke in three areas—definitions of "hospital orderly" and "social worker" and identification of the higher paid occupation as between "janitor" and "policeman." Jordan pupils are more likely to come into contact with the lower levels of service occupations (and, probably, proportionately more likely to have contact with a policeman). In the case of "social worker," a very high proportion of the Jordan student body lives in public housing and in households receiving income from "welfare," and would therefore have frequent occasion to know or observe a County social worker. In this specific instance, precisely the same pattern emerges from the east Los Angeles survey. Students at Roosevelt, Garfield, and other Los Angeles District schools were 100 percent right on the definition of "social worker," while the better off students in non–Los Angeles schools scored markedly lower on this question (more than a third answered incorrectly or said they did not know).

Similarly, as a group, Chicanos showed more knowledge of the definition of "machinist" than did the Blacks. This was the only category in which a majority of the community surveyed failed to answer the knowledge question correctly: almost six tenths of the Blacks either responded incorrectly or said they did not know, while about 63 percent of the Chicanos had the correct answer. Higher percentages of Chicanos than Blacks are or have been employed in the more skilled occupations where there would be some opportunity to observe the work of a "machinist" or even perform in that capacity. Perhaps of equal or greater importance is the fact that Chicanos *generally* penetrate those occupations to a somewhat higher degree than do the Blacks, thereby setting in motion the circular information system described earlier. According to the UES surveys in Los Angeles in 1968–1969, about two thirds of all employed Mexican–American men age 20 and older were semiskilled or skilled, compared to about 54 percent of all employed Negro men in that age group.[3]

Certain of the findings of our survey may be compared to the published results of the Parnes longitudinal study, which includes the lengthier version of the information quiz from which we extracted the eight questions used in our own interview. Both the Parnes study and our own have found that the amount of occupational information tends to grow with age and labor market experience, and that those who were college preparatory majors in school do better in the quiz than those who majored in vocational programs. Our results differ in several respects: most notably, the Parnes study showed a dramatic relationship between knowledge and such variables as educational attainment and vocational training (outside of regular school), while the relationship delineated in our findings is relatively weak or nonexistent. As a whole, high school graduates in our sample do somewhat better than do the dropouts, but the difference in result could hardly be described as dramatic or tremendously consequential. The relationship between training and knowledge is absent in our survey, and in south Los Angeles it sometimes seems to be inverse. Nor is the relationship between knowledge and pay as clear in our findings as it seems to be in the Parnes study. In both the Parnes study and ours, several of the conclusions probably should be regarded as tentative because of sampling size and problems in isolating the causal variables.[4] In interpreting results, of course, the observed differences in samples and in interview schedules should always be kept in mind.

The Parnes study reveals that Black youngsters consistently have less knowledge of the labor market than the Whites, even when adjustments are made for socioeconomic factors such as family income, etc. Our comparisons are only between Blacks and Chicanos in two communities within the Greater Los Angeles area, but again it appears that Blacks obtain less information. Some of the reasons may be suggested by our explorations of certain influences not examined as deeply (or, perhaps, not an-

alyzed in the context of a specific minority community) in the
Parnes study. As indicated before, most of the Chicanos interviewed had discussed jobs with their fathers, and our findings
relative to labor market knowledge show that those young men are
consistently more knowledgeable than their ethnic and age counterparts who had *not* so discussed jobs. In south Los Angeles,
many fewer had discussed jobs with their fathers, and on the
whole, knowledge among those who had is no greater than it is
among those who had not.

In our study labor-market knowledge is most closely connected
in east Los Angeles with advice from the father and other relatives
and friends and with actual labor market experience, and in south
Los Angeles, with help and counsel from friends, experience in
jobs, and contacts with certain public agencies or community
organizations. To the extent that there is some relationship statistically between knowledge and remembrance of guidance classes
and aptitude tests, it does not appear that this has much cause-
and-effect significance. In south Los Angeles, almost everyone in
the survey had had tenth grade guidance (which is required in the
schools they attended) and therefore the fact that those recalling it
generally do better on the information quiz must be the consequence of a separate variable. The answer in part may lie in
differing content of guidance classes at Locke and at Jordan, and
it is of course conceivable that the additional testing and information offered at Locke may have had a positive impact and may
also have caused more youngsters to remember it. However, there
are many other differences between the Locke and Jordan student
bodies, any one of which could explain the observed variations in
knowledge. In general it can perhaps be concluded that the
amount of assistance provided by the guidance class is minimal in
relation to other influences, but that, given the absence of many
other sources in the Watts area, whatever help it offers is worthwhile and necessary.

It is possible that those who are more inclined to recall things
like guidance classes, aptitude tests, HRD contacts, and so on,
simply represent a more sophisticated group of young men whose
knowledge, motivation and awareness have been derived from a
variety of sources independent of education. There is the additional possibility that survey results are skewed according to the
willingness and ability of the respondents to answer these types of

questions fully and accurately and that the survey process itself
has a selective bias in it. As the increasingly reluctant veteran of
formal or informal surveys in low-income areas, I can attest to the
capriciousness of many of the results obtained.

Before proceeding to an examination of other survey findings,
perhaps we should consider some aspects of the knowledge quiz
which may or may not be capricious. I noted earlier that in south
Los Angeles there is a bimodal distribution of responses when
knowledge is cross-tabulated against household income and, with
one exception only, the greatest knowledge is evidenced in the
lower-income (below $4000) and higher-income (above $6000)
groups. This may be a procedural or statistical quirk, or it may
well reflect some underlying relationship between the variables.
Some speculations may be in order. It seems likely that households
receiving the higher income contain persons with greater participation in the labor market, more employment, and probably greater
education and experience. The pattern in the low-income households is more puzzling, but it appears logical that the members of
these households would have more contacts with public agencies,
community organizations, and other programs (such as NYC)
which have eligibility requirements, either *de jure* or *de facto*,
based upon income. Those in the $4000 to $6000 group would
not have either the educational attainment and labor market
experience reflected in the higher-income category or the degree of
contact with "antipoverty" programs as in the lower-income
bracket, though their income is only slightly above the poverty
line. This pattern does not hold true in east Los Angeles, but we
have previously noted that the Chicanos in general have much less
contact with public agencies or community organizations, and
logically the degree of their labor market knowledge would be far
less dependent upon or associated with whatever information
might be derived from those sources.


## Perceptions

Community perceptions of the labor market, as reflected in
estimates of what an average American family *does* and *should*
make over the year, appear to be related to the household income
which already prevails in the immediate neighborhood. In east Los

Angeles, where incomes are higher on the average than they are in Watts (according to our sample), respondents tend to guess higher than in the lower income Black community. As a generalization, it would seem that young men in the communities surveyed usually perceive the average U. S. family income as a notch or two above the income level in their neighborhood, and the *right* income, then, is seen as being at a level correspondingly above the perceived average. In both communities, the modal responses were within the correct bracket ($8000 to $9999 a year), but about 51 percent of the Watts respondents put the average below $8000 compared to only about 38 percent of the Chicanos. Only about one fifth of the east Los Angeles sample fixed the average below $6000, compared to 31 percent of the Blacks.

In east Los Angeles the older (age 20-24) group is more

**Table 8.**

*Perceptions of Average*
*U.S. Family Income, by Age and Area*
(*Percent*)

| Perceived Income | East Los Angeles | | South Los Angeles | |
|---|---|---|---|---|
| | 16-19 | 20-24 | 16-19 | 20-24 |
| Below $4,000 | 9.8 | 11.0 | 14.6 | 9.5 |
| $ 4,000-5,999 | 8.5 | 15.9 | 17.1 | 19.0 |
| $ 6,000-7,999 | 19.6 | 11.0 | 13.0 | 24.8 |
| $ 8,000-9,999 | 22.2 | 30.5 | 26.0 | 19.0 |
| $10,000-11,999 | 22.9 | 20.7 | 13.8 | 11.7 |
| $12,000-13,999 | 3.3 | 6.1 | 6.5 | 6.6 |
| $14,000+ | 10.5 | 4.9 | 5.7 | 8.0 |
| No Idea | 3.3 | 0.0 | 3.3 | 1.5 |

**Table 9.**

*Perceptions of What a Family Should Make,*
*by Age and Area* (*Percent*)

| | East Los Angeles | | South Los Angeles | |
|---|---|---|---|---|
| | 16-19 | 20-24 | 16-19 | 20-24 |
| Below $4,000 | 8.5 | 6.0 | 7.6 | 2.3 |
| $ 4,000-5,999 | 8.5 | 8.4 | 8.4 | 19.5 |
| $ 6,000-7,999 | 16.3 | 14.5 | 13.4 | 18.0 |
| $ 8,000-9,999 | 15.0 | 8.4 | 29.4 | 17.3 |
| $10,000-11,999 | 13.1 | 14.5 | 10.9 | 15.8 |
| $12,000-13,999 | 9.8 | 25.3 | 7.6 | 7.5 |
| $14,000+ | 25.5 | 20.5 | 15.1 | 15.8 |
| No Idea | 3.3 | 2.4 | 7.6 | 3.8 |

accurate in its perception than the younger (age 16-19), while in
south Los Angeles the reverse is true. The Watts young adults
guessed much lower than any other group, with about 53 percent
choosing the below $8000 categories. The east Los Angeles
teenagers tend to guess the highest, with almost 37 percent
estimating $10,000 and above. In east Los Angeles, however, both
age groups concentrate their replies in the $8000 to $12,000
category, whereas the concentration is less in the Watts area.

When we move to an analysis of perceptions related to what the
average income level *should* be, we find that the modal responses
rise in such a way that Blacks concentrate their replies in the
$8000 to $9999 bracket which represents, in fact, the correct
answer to the previous question regarding the actual average. The
mode for the east Los Angeles sample rises even higher, now
located in the above-$14,000 category. Almost half of the Chicano
young adult group identifies the ideal family income at a level in
excess of $12,000. The south Los Angeles perceptions are more
evenly dispersed along the range of incomes, but almost three
tenths of the teenagers think that the appropriate income should
fall in the $8000 to $9999 bracket—precisely where the U.S.
average now lies. Only about 23 percent in each south Los
Angeles age group thinks that the family income should be
$12,000 and above.

The significance of this may lie in its effect upon the career
goals of young men in Watts and east Los Angeles. Such perceptions, for instance, must be viewed in the light of the possible role
of the subeconomy, discussed in Chapter 7. To young men in
low-income neighborhoods, whose perception of a "possible" or
"reasonable" income is obviously affected by their observations
and experience, the income derived from illicit economic activity
must seem impressive when judged in terms of what they think the
average American family does and should make during a year.
Conceivably an improved information system might convince them
that the much safer and more predictable "average" income is
worth the effort in the official labor market.

There is, unfortunately, another side to this picture. All of the
income derived from the subeconomy is "net" to the recipient,
while the regular work income of the American family is taxed
and otherwise encumbered. The young man in the ghetto and
barrio, alert as he is to all possibilities and oriented toward the

present rather than the future, readily detects that the strictly "unofficial" nature of his income sources has its economic advantages in the short run. The inequities in the prevailing tax system only strengthen this conviction. In one case with which the author is directly familiar, a young man in a welfare family went for many years without any income except for what he occasionally earned through NYC, and then in one recent year, having managed to obtain a "permanent" custodial job which lasted until he was laid off as the result of an unfortunate mishap, he earned over $7000. His income tax return was professionally prepared (of course, at a cost to him) and was subsequently checked by the author, but the IRS computer determined, without explanation and seemingly without reason, that he was not entitled to his claimed refund and that, to the contrary, the amounts withheld were not even sufficient to cover the tax owed. Though he had had very little income prior to that tax year and has had virtually no income since, he cannot take advantage of the "income averaging" privileges granted to the more affluent and is forced to pay what seems to be an excessively high tax when others in much higher and more consistent income brackets (including, at the state tax level, the Governor of California) often pay nothing. Though he is an extremely responsible and conscientious youngster, it would be difficult to convince him (and even more difficult to persuade his brothers and friends and associates) that honest work pays off.[5]

The major results of our inquiry into the labor market preferences of young men in Watts and east Los Angeles suggest that their goals and values are well in line with those held by the majority of Americans, and that any subsequent failure to realize their ambitions will be the consequence of lack of opportunity rather than of alienation. The majority in both east and south Los Angeles believe that their best interests would be served by finishing school and then proceeding directly into full-time employment. About 48 percent of the Blacks and 42 percent of the Chicanos would prefer (if they could) to complete college before beginning regular work. About 12 percent of the Blacks and 9.5 percent of the Chicanos prefer to enter special vocational training before working, and about 7 and 5 percent respectively check the suggested work and education combination. Immediate employment, with night school on their own time, is preferred by 12 percent of Blacks and 4.5 percent of Chicanos. A bare 6 percent of Blacks and 9 percent of Chicanos think it is best to begin their work careers without further education or training.

It is interesting that this general pattern, with high preference ratings given to further education, holds true for virtually all the subcategories of respondents included in our cross–tabulations. Dropouts, for example, rate further education and training highly, except that tenth grade dropouts in Watts are less inclined to check "college." The education plus work combination appeals to a high percentage (14.3 percent) of Locke students, and surprisingly a higher percentage of Jordan than Locke students think that finishing college would be preferable to terminating education with the diploma. Service and unskilled workers in both areas rate education (and specifically college) very high, and both low-paid and high-paid workers agree on this same preference. One minor difference between areas is that the college preference is strongest in the $6000-plus household income group in south Los Angeles and in the below-$4000 group in east Los Angeles. There is also a somewhat greater inclination in east Los Angeles to enter the permanent labor force without a college education.

In retrospect, the "preference" questions probably could have been worded and cast in a better form which would highlight the alternatives more clearly. Their position toward the end of the interview schedule was undoubtedly a deterrent to adequate and more meaningful response. I suspect, as I commented earlier, that a higher percentage of the samples would prefer the combination work–education plan if it were presented in clearer and more emphatic fashion, and unfortunately it was probably perceived by many respondents as an alternative to the regular college education rather than as a way of combining that education (or other education) with employment.

Nevertheless, even with these qualifications and defects, the survey does effectively emphasize what Professor Seeman has argued: that the poor (and specifically the minority poor) share many of the key values and aspirations held by the majority of Americans. If there is a "culture of poverty" characterized by alienation and hostility to educational and other valued goals, it does not emerge from our survey results. This, of course, may simply reflect the limitations of the formal survey process. Personal observation, however, tends to confirm these statistical findings, and other parts of the survey, including the inquiry into career choice, provide further corroborative evidence. The next chapter examines this evidence and its implications for the long-term role of Blacks and Chicanos in the American economy.

NOTES

1. *Career Thresholds*, Vol. 1, February 1969.

2. See, e.g., "Learning and Doing in American Society," by Jerome Rosow, Occasional Paper No. 1, Manpower Research Center, Institute of Industrial Relations, UCLA.

3. BLS Regional Report No. 14, January 1970, p. 22.

4. See *Career Thresholds*, Volume 1, Chapter V, pp. 119-138.

5. Bruno Stein, in his recent book *On Relief*, argues that poor households pay higher taxes than they should (especially in relation to the amounts paid by higher-income households) and makes a number of suggestions for equalizing the tax burden more fairly.

Unless otherwise indicated, all income and tax figures and other financial references in this chapter relate to the year 1970.

# 6

## CHOOSING A CAREER

The message emerging from our study of career choice in east Los Angeles and Watts is clear and unmistakable: Most Black and Brown young men in low-income ghettos and barrios want professional or other white-collar careers, if they have the power to choose. The preference transcends all boundaries and cuts across the spectrum of incomes, jobs, labor market status, and almost every relevant variable. Some are more optimistic than others about their prospects for attainment of that goal, but, incontrovertibly, they share with the Anglo working and middle class a strong interest in and proclivity toward the white-collar occupations. Ranked second behind "professional" in order of preference, to be sure, is skilled labor, but this is much farther down the scale. Noticeable proportions of youngsters surveyed are interested in careers with business or government, the Blacks opting more often for the former and the Chicanos for the latter.

As a whole, the Blacks in our sample tend to be "education oriented," a tendency reflected in the percentages of Black youngsters who said merely that they wanted to complete their education

## Table 10.
### *Career Choice, by Age and Area*
#### (*Percent*)

|  | East Los Angeles | | South Los Angeles | |
|---|---|---|---|---|
|  | *16-19* | *20-24* | *16-19* | *20-24* |
| Unknown | 26.5 | 20.5 | 18.0 | 7.1 |
| School | — | — | 6.6 | 2.9 |
| Professional, N.E.C. | 33.1 | 36.1 | 28.7 | 37.9 |
| Skilled | 14.6 | 8.4 | 15.6 | 15.0 |
| Business | 1.3 | 6.0 | 7.4 | 8.6 |
| Government | 7.9 | 6.0 | 2.5 | 1.4 |
| Music, art, etc | 4.0 | 2.4 | 3.3 | 3.6 |
| Entertainment | 1.3 | 1.2 | 2.5 | 3.6 |
| Unskilled | — | — | — | — |
| Clerical | 0.0 | 1.2 | 1.6 | 4.3 |
| Medical (nonprofessional) | 1.3 | 0.0 | 4.1 | 2.1 |
| Sports, etc. | 2.0 | 4.8 | 1.6 | 2.9 |
| Semiskilled | 0.7 | 3.6 | 2.5 | 1.4 |
| Service | 2.0 | 3.6 | 0.8 | 3.6 |
| Political, etc. | 0.0 | 3.6 | 0.0 | 1.4 |
| Other | 2.0 | 0.0 | 0.8 | 2.1 |
| Combination | 0.7 | 0.0 | 1.6 | 0.0 |
| Unable to code | 2.6 | 2.4 | 2.5 | 2.1 |

before deciding on a career. The semiskilled, service and clerical fields interest small proportions of the young men, an intriguing and provocative result in the light of the fact that many established training programs are focused primarily upon those very occupations. I shall have occasion later to comment upon the importance of this finding.

The preference for a professional career (and indeed the entire order of preference) tends to be unaffected by variables such as family income, amount of counseling, labor market status, educational attainment, type of work held, school attended, whether the respondent had been in a training program or whether he had discussed jobs with his father. By and large, the expressed interest in skilled occupations is no greater in east than in south Los Angeles (and there is even some evidence that it is less in the Chicano community surveyed).

"Yeah, they gave us a test. Very seldom, you would get your results. You know, you take all the tests and you never would get the results, so I know I took one test. The whole school took this test. It's a vocational aptitude test. And I was considered mechanically inclined. In other words, I was supposed to wind up being like working in a factory. All the tests showed was, like, putting things together and stuff like that. But that's not all; I mean, anybody would like to put things together. But that don't mean that's their ultimate. And so what happened, they put me in an industrial major" (Alfred Jackson).

About 5 percent of the teenagers in each area are interested in some phase of cultural or entertainment activity, and the proportion rises somewhat within the age 20-24 group in south Los Angeles. Interest in most other occupations is scattered, and proportionately marginal. Needless to say, there is no preference whatsoever for the unskilled trades.

When we review the cross tabulations between career choice and family income, the pattern is unchanged. Indeed, in east Los Angeles the residents of below-$6000 households display a greater proportionate interest in professional careers than do those of above-$6000 households. In south Los Angeles we can observe the same bimodal pattern which has appeared in other tabulations: the ambitions for a professional career are greatest at the income extremes, with comparatively more persons in the $4000 to $6000 household category indicating an interest in the skilled trades or expressing no choice at all.

The relative community preferences vis-à-vis careers in business or government are somewhat puzzling because they seem to be the reverse of the actual employment pattern in the east Los Angeles and Watts communities. Proportionately more Chicanos than Blacks prefer careers in government, whereas relatively more of the Blacks are inclined toward business careers. The employment figures, however, show that the Blacks surveyed have penetrated government jobs to a greater degree than have the Chicanos. Perhaps the experience has been disillusioning, at least in terms of the pay levels attained or observed. Blacks may be relatively more interested in business careers because they perceive that these jobs are better paid, while the Chicanos have not yet had sufficient experience to justify that perception.

A not inconsiderable number of young Chicanos expressed an interest in becoming probation or correctional officers, due possibly to their observations and contacts. The Blacks rarely articulated such a preference, whatever their private feelings may be. My own past knowledge of the vocational interests of young men in these areas suggests that many are intrigued by employment possibilities in this field, provided they are not required to serve as policemen on the local beat. They have little admiration for policemen as a group, but would not hesitate to accept work as a bailiff or marshal in a courtroom, a probation or parole officer, or a jailer.[1]

The reasons advanced for these various career choices (professional, skilled labor, entertainment, etc.) are varied but tend to fall in amorphous classifications such as "interest," "observation," "experience," and so forth. The only clearcut conclusion to be drawn from this part of the survey is that "counseling and testing" have had minimal impact upon the process of selection. The chief effect of counseling, to the degree that it has any effect at all, is to strengthen the young man's motivation to continue his schooling and not enter the labor market too quickly. The results here merely confirm our prior findings that vocational guidance is of little or no value in affecting career choice.

Though the reason was not enunciated as frankly or as often as one might have expected, certainly the possibility of high earnings is a substantial consideration in the selection of a career. I suspect that, at this moment, motivations of this type may be stronger and more socially acceptable in these communities than they are among similar age groups in the higher-income Anglo areas. The young man in a ghetto or barrio has no "hang-ups" about making money, an opportunity which historically has been denied to him and his ethnic compatriots. Clearly the youngsters interviewed expect to earn good money from their chosen occupation. Approximately 60 percent in each area would expect to make $10,000 a year or more in a "professional" career. In east Los Angeles, about that same percentage would apply in the case of those choosing a skilled trade, and although the Watts sample is not quite as optimistic as this, most of the respondents in this category expect to earn an income equal to or above the median family income in the United States.

Partly from personal observation and partly from survey findings, I would infer that the process of a long, sustained career effort ("starting at the bottom and working your way to the top") is of little practical or realistic meaning to many minority youngsters in low-income ghettos. Aside from sources such as the subeconomy, large incomes are perceived as deriving from a combination of natural talent, luck, and "connections." In describing the process, many ghetto youngsters will use the phrase "getting over," their equivalent of the Anglo expression "getting ahead." While it is easily possible to make too much of such semantic differences, I am inclined to think that the two expressions convey different perceptions. The Anglo phrase implies a process in which hard work, ambition, and "playing the game" are regularly rewarded over time, while "to get over" connotes the climbing of a barrier or the bridging of a gap separating two distinct economies or life styles.

Certainly the process of income attainment varies substantially in the established labor market, and some of the variations would seem to have more significance for ghetto or barrio youngsters than would others. For instance, fields such as entertainment or sports are characterized, at least on the surface, by wide gaps between the highest and lowest incomes, with the higher-income levels sometimes attained quickly and at a young age (perhaps necessarily, in the light of the requirements of the field). In some cases, such as professional sports, it might be inferred that the performer either receives a high income or none at all, and success or failure would often seem to be instantaneous. Thus athletes or young musical groups such as the Jackson Five or Santana offer the most immediate and visible examples of what is possible with talent and a lot of luck. They have "gotten over," in some cases proceeding directly from near poverty to great wealth.[2]

On the other hand, to a greater degree than I would have imagined, the young men in our samples evidenced a considerable awareness of the special preparation or the prerequisites attached to the careers they preferred. Among those who prefer "professional" or "skilled" or "government" occupations, for example, it is widely recognized that some combination of general education and special training is required. Only in the very small east Los Angeles "clerical" sample is there a pervasive belief that no more than a high school education is needed as a precondition for successful entry into the preferred career. Otherwise, only in the "semiskilled" category does this percentage equal as much as one third (in east Los Angeles) and one quarter (in south Los Angeles).

Furthermore, those who prefer the professions typically show substantial knowledge of the labor market, with some variations. In east Los Angeles this pattern is rather consistent, but in Watts the group preferring professional work has some trouble defining the blue-collar jobs of "hospital orderly" and "machinist." Generally too, those who prefer "skilled labor" demonstrate a high level of labor market knowledge. Relatively the least knowledge seems to be displayed by those who have not decided on a career goal or prefer simply to complete school before deciding.

Though a much higher proportion of the east Los Angeles sample had discussed jobs with their fathers, the evidence suggests that among those who had had such a discussion, its influence upon career choice may have been somewhat greater in south Los Angeles than in east Los Angeles. There are minor differences in east Los Angeles, with slightly lower percentages of "discussants" choosing professional and skilled occupations and a somewhat higher proportion choosing government work, but the more marked difference occurs in the Watts area. There, a much greater uncertainty about career preference is evidenced by those who had *not* discussed jobs, and higher preferences for professional and business careers are stated by the "yes" group. Indeed, when the "undecideds" are eliminated from that group, somewhat over half of those making a choice prefer professional work or business. Again it must be remembered that the majority in Watts had never discussed careers with their fathers at all.

When we turn to the question of how the various respondents perceive their chances of succeeding in their career aspirations, variations appear. Among those still in school, the college students are most optimistic. High school graduates (who have not entered college) are usually more optimistic than dropouts, but here we find that notable percentages of graduates will respond "fair" or "poor" or "no idea." There is no evidence that contacts with counselors have any relationship to these perceptions, but those who recall taking a guidance class or aptitude test tend to be somewhat more optimistic than do those who have no such recollection. It is difficult to know whether this has any real significance.

Two variables in particular seem to have a rather strong relationship to perceptions of success in pursuing career goals: family income and labor market status. In both areas those in the highest-income households are more optimistic than their poorer associates. About half of those in $6000-plus households think their chances are "very good" or "good." However, the most pessimistic group in east Los Angeles by far is in the *middle* ($4000 to $6000) income category. Almost two thirds of this category in east Los Angeles, and two fifths in Watts, consider their chances "fair" or "poor" or "impossible." By contrast the corresponding percentages for the below–$4000 groups are about 37 percent among Chicanos and 48 percent among Blacks.

It should be noted, in addition, that high percentages of those in the $6000-plus household income category label their chances "fair," "poor," or "impossible," or have no idea what their prospects might be. This is particularly evident in south Los Angeles, where a majority of the respondents (55 percent) in this category are less than optimistic about their chances. In sum, those in better-off households are inclined to be more optimistic than those who are worse off, but across the board there remain many who are dubious or uncertain.

By and large, the employed are much more optimistic than the unemployed, a relationship which is expected and seems to make sense. One qualification is that high percentages of employed persons also have no definite notion as to what their chances are of achieving their goal. Those who are in unskilled or semiskilled occupations are least optimistic about their prospects, while those many in the service categories seem reasonably hopeful.

The pattern among those in school differs somewhat by area. In south Los Angeles the students are rather strongly optimistic, with 60 percent describing their chances as "very good" or "good" and only 7.5 percent regarding them as "poor" or "impossible." The students in east Los Angeles are not so optimistic: almost 43 percent consider their prospects only "fair." Another 18 percent label them "poor" and nearly 11 percent have no idea at all. Obviously much depends upon whether the respondent thinks he can successfully make it through school, since many of those surveyed (especially in the Watts area) associate their potential for success with the quality and quantity of their education. This seems to be a realistic appraisal where aspirations are focused upon professional and other white-collar occupations. In both areas the university students are by far the most optimistic: about three quarters view their chances as "very good" or "good."

As suggested earlier, effective counseling is absent in most schools examined, but the Anglo youngsters receive and accept a great deal of guidance or information from their parents. In south

Los Angeles most of the young men get little or no career counseling from their fathers, and although the Chicano youngsters are proportionately more likely to discuss jobs within the household, there are no particularly significant differences in career preference between those who do and those who do not.

One factor may be that young men in both areas show relatively little interest in pursuing their fathers' lines of work. This lack of interest is even more pronounced in east than in south Los Angeles, which may help explain why so many of the youngsters seem unaffected by their discussions with parents. Thus a source of information and guidance which appears important in Anglo communities does not have much visible impact in the areas we have surveyed.

It would seem that the relative absence of this source in low-income minority communities would require a correspondingly greater effort by schools, public agencies, and community organizations to fill the gap. Our study has uncovered no evidence that this is the case in Watts or east Los Angeles. The training programs have had a minimal effect, and even suffer from a low visibility among many of the young men to whom presumably they are directed. The Employment Service offers little in the way of meaningful information or counseling. The Los Angeles City Schools require a guidance class in the tenth grade, but its substance varies considerably among schools, and as a whole, neither students nor teachers consider it effective as a source of career data and most of the young men interviewed cannot even recall it. In many schools standard aptitude or interest inventory tests are given, but the results are generally given little weight in the subsequent academic counseling process.

There is of course a fundamental question as to whether "career counseling" has any relevance at all in the context of the attitudes and goals of young people and the complexities of the labor market. While the structure of jobs expands and fragments (the *Dictionary of Occupational Titles* has 21,741 entries, an increase of about 6000 over the previous edition published five years earlier), the interest in "careers" as traditionally viewed has appeared to decline among young men generally. The counterreaction, in its most pervasive and visible form, expresses a broad rejection of the principle that self-aggrandizement automatically serves the best interest of society at the same time (a basic tenet of classical economics) and that ambition for material gain or status is a desirable or acceptable value. My own perception is that this "rebellion" against materialism is more an aspect of middle-class than of low-income youth culture. To be sure, many young men in the ghetto and barrio have also avoided the traditional "career" route to material success, but much of their resistance has been directed against the means rather than the end. As argued elsewhere in this study, they would like an opportunity to share in some of the benefits of affluence before rejecting it as the Anglo middle-class youngsters now appear to do. Nor is it yet clear that they would reject "careers" *if* this were a visible and realistic alternative for them.

The related question is whether secondary education should continue to be strongly oriented toward the academically inclined college-bound student, or should give greater emphasis to the needs of youngsters who will enter the labor market after completing high school.[3] This question can arouse passionate reactions, especially in those areas where "voc ed" has historically been a dumping ground for students regarded as unteachable or otherwise unsuited for further education. Many minority parents have protested strongly that their children are categorized as "vocational" rather than "college preparatory" students, thus denying them the additional educational opportunities to which they are entitled. Others—administrators, educators, and community residents alike—will argue that secondary education in general is now excessively oriented toward the "better," college-bound pupil and insufficiently attentive to the requirements of the large number who will never be college graduates.

The present U. S. Commissioner of Education, Sidney Marland, Jr., has called for an overhauling of vocational education at both high school and college levels, with the purpose of improving the process by which broad career decisions are made and implemented. Stating the case for a reinvigorated vacationally oriented curriculum which will be realistic and flexible and will offer students a number of meaningful career options, the *Wall Street Journal* has editorially argued that:

The drift away from career orientation in education—at the college level as well as the high school level—may well be partly responsible for some of the confusion and frustration that afflict many young people. To introduce stronger encouragement to think in career terms at a younger age may well help to restore a sense of purpose among young people who now lack such a sense.

But perhaps most important is the possibility that introduction of career orientation in secondary education will remove some of the damaging stigma that attaches to pursuit of careers that do not involve college training. There can be little doubt that this stigma has caused too many students to drift aimlessly into college when they could have been spending their time more usefully training for other pursuits.

This drift has several undesirable effects. It may discourage the individual from developing his or her best talents or skills. It denies needed talents and skills to the economy. The presence of aimless students on college campuses dilutes the efforts of the colleges to provide first-rate education to those students with a genuine academic bent.

In other words, the present system is highly inefficient if we are to assume that one role of education should be to prepare people for a useful role in the economy as well as a responsible role as citizens. To fill that role some educators will have to adopt some new attitudes toward their task. There also will be some considerable expense in developing the curricula, teachers, and laboratories for this purpose.

Even so, if the fruits of such an effort will be to improve the skill level and productivity of the economy, to create greater job satisfactions for a wider number of people and to remove some of the class and status considerations that have attached themselves to work, the effort will have been well worth making.[4]


In principle, the recommendations of the *Journal* editorial are unexceptionable, but serious dangers lurk in the background if the move toward expanded vocational training and career orientation is not properly implemented and controlled. There are now fundamental defects in the process by which youngsters are tested and counseled and the "academic" students identified and separated from the "vocational." Few schools have innovated in this area; testing instruments often remain unvalidated and even unreviewed; and, as we have seen through our survey, students are given little information on which to base rational choices. The structure of post-secondary education itself demands reevaluation and renovation, with further experimentation in fields such as accelerated and part-time degree programs, school/work experience combinations, and special educational curricula directed to the interests and needs of youngsters from low-income areas.

This latter point is of special significance to our study of career aspirations in south and east Los Angeles, because the lack of clearly visible and attainable alternatives either in education or the labor market has caused many young men to drift into what we have termed the subeconomy. Served neither by the schools nor by the market, they have entered a marginal and ill-defined territory where short-run needs are satisfied at the expense of their long-run personal development. We shall explore this territory in the next chapter.

NOTES

1. In defining our occupational classifications, we assigned all such occupations to the "government work" category because they are unique to government and exist nowhere else. In the case of "social worker," we assigned that to the "professional" category because it can and does exist in private agencies, though it would occur most often in government employment.

2. I hasten to emphasize that this often has more the appearance than the substance of reality, because in many cases the currently "successful" performer has spent a long and unrewarding apprenticeship ("paying his dues") before finally achieving his success.

3. There is a highly articulate school of thought, represented by spokesmen such as Robert Maynard Hutchins, which argues that the purpose of education is and should remain entirely unrelated to vocational goals and should concentrate upon liberal arts and analytical training to develop the well rounded and intellectually strong citizen.

4. *Wall Street Journal*, September 13, 1971, p. 12. See also "Learning to Earn," *Newsweek*, August 30, 1971, pp. 74-75, for a discussion of innovative programs in vocational education and further comments by Commissioner Marland.

# 7

## THE SUBECONOMY

The relative lack of attention paid to the economic significance of illegal markets in the ghetto and barrio (and elsewhere in the economy) is a measure of the distance of many academicians from social reality. To the extent that it has been recognized at all in recent years, this income-producing activity has usually been treated as peripheral or of unknown and speculative impact. Prescriptions for social policy and analyses of economic issues, affecting those who live in the inner city, are regularly issued without the slightest consideration given to the realities of daily life among those most directly involved.

Rather than being marginal or of uncertain importance, the subeconomy is probably the greatest single source of market income for young men in the central city. The participants in Watts, for example, estimate that they obtain equally as much income from this source as from all the governmental programs combined. "Just about as much money in the community illegally as it is that the government is funding. Go back to that saying when you cop a kilo [of marijuana], you cop three or four kilos, you do your thing, you know, you make that much money—that's dishonest money, so they say. Can you just go right offhand and tell me how much money the government put into Watts so far" (George—south Los Angeles)?

This admittedly subjective impression seems to be confirmed by recent findings and reports of congressional committees and government agencies. The magnitude of illegal economic activity in the production and sale of drugs alone is staggering: more than two years ago the House Select Committee on Crime estimated that 8 *billion* amphetamine pills are produced every year in the United States, and "Federal officials estimate that *no more than half of this production is routinely dispensed through doctors' prescriptions*" (emphasis added).[1] This, of course, is just one of the many types of drugs which are regularly distributed in east Los Angeles and Watts; others are barbiturates, Seconal tablets ("red devils" and "yellow jackets"), tranquilizers, less commonly LSD, and several more.

The sale of marijuana is also "big business." The same House committee has estimated that 12 million Americans have tried marijuana and that as many as 31 percent of teenagers may be users. The committee believes that the annual expenditure for the use of marijuana amounts to approximately $850 million, a figure which some of us regard as quite conservative. Throughout the world about 250 million people have used marijuana or hashish (the latter is, like marijuana, a product of the cannabis plant and reputedly is somewhat stronger in its effect).[2]

The income from traffic in "hard drugs" (heroin, cocaine, opium, morphine, etc.) is even more impressive, though the risk is great and this industry is so highly organized that little of the revenue filters down to the young men of Watts and east Los Angeles. Approximately 1.5 tons of heroin are imported into the United States annually, producing an income of more than $300 million each year. The heroin distributor in Harlem will earn a clear profit of about $30,000 a week, and the street peddlers will be given commissions for selling packets of heroin at $25 apiece.[3]

For our purposes, the subeconomy (or street economy) can be defined as a market for the distribution of goods and services which are in demand but have been outlawed officially for social or moral reasons. Thus it would encompass the production, sale, and consumption of both "hard" and "soft" drugs; gambling;

illegal betting and "numbers"; prostitution and pimping; and similar activities. This definition excludes income-producing activities such as theft or the sale of stolen property, for the reason that these represent a forced and involuntary redistribution of property rather than the original production and sale of goods in response to existing market demand. Further, these latter forms of income production have been made illegal for reasons extending beyond the desire to regulate private morals; in short, they involve "victims."

I have also chosen to concentrate upon the markets for marijuana and pills, because observation suggests that these are the major sources of continuing income for young men in the areas which I have examined. In addition, my impression is that the consumption of those products is pervasive, whereas the market for hard drugs is much more limited in scope, and, pragmatically, research into the hard narcotics trade (controlled as it is by organized crime) is fraught with peril.

Though the bulk of economic analysis, such as that concerned with the employment effects of minimum wages, continues to ignore the subeconomy, some economists have recently expressed an awareness of it. Peter Doeringer has noted that job-seekers in the ghetto have a list of "preferred" employers, as a counterpart to the rankings of "preferred" employees which form the basis for the "queue theory" of labor market demand. Therefore they are not always available for the menial, low-paid jobs which typically are offered to unskilled youngsters or, perhaps, stay on such jobs only for short periods. One reason for this, he suggests, is that "the social systems of the ghetto are compatible with turnover. Alternatives to earned income, for example, are available from welfare programs, hustling, and income sharing among friends and relatives, so that ghetto workers can easily withhold their labor services for short periods of time, or treat work as a supplementary source of income. In addition, the active social life of the ghetto, much of it centered on the street, can compete with work as a regular activity."[4]

In his analysis of income transfer systems and their possible effect on labor force participation, Bruno Stein has observed, perceptively, that "most writers omit illicit activity from their analysis, although 'hustling' and other forms of making-do are not unknown among the poor. Crime for profit is part of the American economy, although it is not included in data on the gross national product. It is probably a significant part of what may be termed net ghetto income, but data are equally lacking."[5]

The 1971 *Manpower Report of the President* gives perhaps the most explicit explanation of the key role of the subeconomy. Based on unpublished interviews with unemployed young persons in Harlem, ages 18 to 24, it concludes that many Black youngsters see the street economy as the only visible and attainable route to some degree of economic success, even though they share many of the generally accepted goals such as education, independence, and social status. The words of the *Report* deserve quotation in full:

> The absence of employment opportunities which could lead to a radical improvement in life styles and movement out of the slums seemed to be the basic reason why jobs, even those which pay above the minimum wage, were sometimes regarded disdainfully. The young people interviewed had little hope of significant increases in earnings, because they saw so little chance of an occupational breakthrough. At best they expected marginal employment at wages which would allow them to "get by." The incentive to work hard in order to effect a major change in their way of life was absent.
>
> Hustling was often regarded as a logical and rational option. The market for gambling, numbers, prostitution, and narcotics is large and highly profitable, and the possibility of "being on one's own" competes powerfully with the opportunities available in the regulated middle-class world.
>
> Criminal activities and the possible handicap of an arrest record did not seem to present problems for these Harlem youth. Issues of this kind were not even raised during the interviews. This finding suggests that the costs attached to engaging in illegal activities tend to be low. No great social stigma accompanies arrest, so far as the immediate neighborhood is concerned. Job opportunities are already limited by other barriers, so that the effect of an arrest record is not considered important. The probability of being apprehended is considered relatively small. And the penalty for a particular offense, if one is caught, can be calculated with reasonable accuracy. Thus, an individual engaged in hustling is usually aware of the chance he is taking.
>
> To gage the impact of illegal activities on the participation of slum residents in the regular labor market, the unemployment rates for workers in the slums of 16 cities were

correlated with crime rates in these cities in 1966. Unemployment was found to be lowest in the cities with the greatest amount of property crime. It appears that the larger the sources of illegal income, the fewer the people in the slums who persist in looking for legitimate jobs (or the greater the numbers who report themselves as employed when they are not, in order to explain their style of life to the enumerators).[6]

### The Structure of the Subeconomy

The process for distributing marijuana—also called "weed," "grass," "pot," and many other names—and pills in Watts and east Los Angeles is reasonably well structured, though it appears to be less highly organized and controlled than the trade in hard narcotics. For both economic and personal reasons the young men whom I interviewed prefer to deal in marijuana rather than pills, though pills (and of course liquor) will be sought and distributed whenever "grass" is unavailable. The market for marijuana is seen as virtually insatiable, while the demand for pills is less pervasive and some of the youngsters have qualms about both the quality and the effect of "red devils" and similar drugs.

Asked about the extent of the market for marijuana in the Watts area, the interviewees were explicit in their responses: "Everybody do it! Eight to eighty. You'd actually be surprised 'cuz some of the people you say, 'well, he seems not to be getting high' and you turn around and that same John Doe is on his back. That's where all the green [money] flows. With the pills you can do it too, but it takes a longer process."

They prefer handling and using marijuana rather than pills because they regard pills as more dangerous and uncertain in quality, and it also appears that the profit is higher and surer with marijuana. "How do they get pills over here, enough pills so even if it was cool, you know, to provide everybody else? You even have cats manufacturing their own. Well, what's the cat been putting in the pills, you know, maybe rat poison? It might even be baking soda—I just lost a dollar or something like that. You know you have second thoughts, that's why I don't buy barbiturates no more. Do you want a $5 bag [of marijuana] or 5 [rolls of] reds? Instead of red devils you buy the weed first, you know a cat don't want to be all juiced up, laying up, reds slowing down your reactions; you know, you might as well be asleep."

"With pills you can't control your high. With whites [amphetamines] you take two, you know, it might not be enough; with three you're out of it."

"The cat may have bought three rolls of red devils from you, which is nine red devils, nine Seconals altogether.[7] He may come back to your house and, say, the cat is dead on your doorstep, and what are you going to do, what's going to happen to you" (Robert)?

Sometimes the same person will deal in both marijuana and pills, but the youngsters state that this is usually considered unwise because it may "mess up your business" for the various reasons already suggested. According to one interviewee, women are more likely to consume and deal in pills than are men ("The red devil is like a spanish fly to a young lady") and have less control over their "high," but whether this is an objective evaluation or an example of male chauvinism is a controversial question on which I fully intend to remain neutral.

The income produced through the sale of marijuana is substantial, provided that the seller can obtain sufficient quantities of the merchandise. "To start with marijuana you can get singles, bags, matchboxes, keys [kilos]. But a single of marijuana is fifty cents you know, which is a cigarette, then there are $5, $10 bags. The size of the bags vary from 13 joints to about 26 joints, you know, depending on who you got the shit from. 'Cause they're going to get you, you know, skimpy bags, switch bags on you. . . . Then when you start dealing with the keys it starts running $100 and up, something like that" (Charles and Robert).

When the dealer can establish access to large quantities, he expects to make a 100 percent untaxed profit on his investment: "You double your money mostly, then you'll make extra money too. If you pay $130, $140—you'll double that. Yeah, you'll at least double your money and still make some. You'll get about $300 if you pay $135, depending upon what size. That's what you're looking for when you first go take care of the business. Right on. They will tell you that you will at least double your money and possibly you might make more. But at the most even if you don't double your money back, you *will* make your money back and plus just about double your money, but you'll come out ahead. But that's not including the risk—like you going to jail" (Willard and Charles).

All the youngsters emphasize the critical importance of *timing* in the business of selling marijuana and pills. The process is closely tied to the social life of the ghetto and barrio, which is at its highest pitch on weekends and special occasions such as parties and festivals. If the supplies and connections are adequate, large profits can be made at those times when many people will be expecting to relax and celebrate. Marijuana, in particular, supposedly heightens the pleasure derived from music, sex, eating, and other concomitants of relaxation. Hence it is important to be able to supply the plentiful demand during these peak periods. The following dialogue between three interviewees from Watts and myself will illustrate some of these points:

*PB*: Let's say that things are going pretty good and you've got kind of good connections. . . . Maybe within a range but figuring the things together, how much can you make on the average a month?

*Willard*: Man, I'd say close to 1, 2, 3 thousand dollars.

*PB*: Are you talking about Watts?

*Willard and Charles*: Yeah, of course. For any individual it shouldn't take you no longer than a week—you got four weeks to get rid of a whole kilo. Well, you got four weeks in a month—let's say you go and cop two times, twice two weeks—the cat may put in an extra half pound for you coming back, taking care of the business for him by bringing your particular business to him. That's your money out there constantly stacking up on you. How frequently, how fast you'll be able to work for this certain person—it's not getting caught that's the point, not the marijuana really that you look at in the long run—the timing, the timing.

*PB*: What do you mean by that?

*Charles*: Let's say, the Watts [Summer] Festival is coming and John Doe wants to sell what's-his-name and you go up there and sell it at the festival and J.D. got his "key" too, doing his thing.

*PB*: Well, I mean, going back, how much could you make?

*Willard*: Well, it shouldn't take you very long. It should take at least two days—no longer than two or three days. During the whole Watts Festival you could make yourself at least about $3000/$4000. Normally, automatically, the first day you're going to make a lot of money because the Watts Festival is sort of like a big thing and everybody would like to get intoxicated.

*Robert*: Yeah, they want to be under the influence. A lot depends on location, too.

*PB*: Who are you really selling to? At the Watts Festival maybe you're selling to a lot of outsiders?

*Willard*: No, no! It's not what you do—it's who you know. The people are sort of particular. See, if they don't know you, they don't do business with you.

*Charles*: Then, again, if your connections are very good even the person that you, say, cop from, they can line you up with a little area and he may buy you up for about $400, $500 in one area. One area, one area in a small bit of time. You know, they can line you up like that—hey, man, you know, something's happening at a place at a certain time and this is where you go.

*Robert*: And a lot depends, you know, I know a cat he makes a living—he makes at least like a hundred dollars from like, you know, the weekend. That's when it really raises. . . . I'm talking about the location I live in. . . . One knocks at the door, one leaving, one coming—man, that's money. I seen a cat make at the most, like on a Friday, $130 for one day, no tax deducted money. Cash money, cash money.

The somewhat unique feature of the subeconomy is that the street dealers generally perform both as sellers and consumers of the product which they purvey. Depending upon timing and circumstances, the same person will be primarily a buyer at one time and predominantly a seller at another. Their reactions to price and quality changes must therefore be schizophrenic, since what they gain as buyers they must then lose as sellers and vice versa. Again, as they point out, timing and connections are critical in determining how they fare economically and personally in this perpetually active and volatile market.

*PB*: I was thinking—you were talking up in the thousands of dollars and one question that comes into somebody's mind —in Watts, who has that kind of money?

*Charles*: Five dollars adds up from everybody. Money, for

instance, like one time there may be five or ten people dealing at the same time. But then . . .

*PB*: Sometimes the dude may be buying and other times he's selling?

*Charles*: That's how he starts off.

*Willard*: Like a cat that may have a kilo last week may come to you for a bag this week.

*PB*: One time, one month of the year somebody will have a kilo and so the buyers will go to him and pretty soon the buyers, they'll be selling it. So the money just keeps circulating around within the framework of the area?

*Robert*: The money's still in the area, but you don't benefit much. Them cats are buying cars and freaking off them pills and stuff, but it'll stay in the area for a time.

These conversations again suggest the nature of the marketing structure for the subeconomy. There appear to be three entrepreneurial levels in a local community: (1) the street dealers, mostly young men who consistently demand the product and at some times, depending on luck and skill and other circumstances, will also sell it; (2) the "middlemen," usually older than the teenagers, for whom this is probably a full time operation, and who serve as the contact points within the particular marketing area, and (3) the top-level "businessmen" who arrange to bring in the supplies of marijuana and pills and distribute them to the various areas. Allied with the middlemen and the businessmen are the political, legal, and law enforcement representatives who provide protection in return for a direct or indirect share of the profits.[8]

## The Elasticity of Demand and Supply

According to the consistent and unanimous statements of young men interviewed, the demand for marijuana should be viewed as highly inelastic while the demand for pills is considerably more elastic and probably would fall off steeply if the price of "reds," for example, rose relative to that of marijuana. Their attachment to marijuana is so strong that they are already willing to run great risks and pay large amounts in order to obtain it, and in general they do not regard either pills or alcohol as being perfectly substitutable for it. Thus if their comments are to be taken literally, the cross-elasticity between the demand for marijuana and that for other products producing an allegedly similar effect must be perceived as low.

Any evaluation of demand elasticity is, of course, rendered much more complex and uncertain by the fact that the street dealers are both consumers *and* sellers of the product, as indicated previously. Any given change in price or quality, therefore, must be viewed in the light of its income as well as its specific demand effect. If any one person is *equally* a seller and a buyer over a given period of time (admittedly an unlikely circumstance, at least in such precise terms), any change in the variables presumably would leave him in relatively the same economic position as before. The more realistic premise is that at any given moment some youngsters are mainly sellers while others (probably the majority) are predominantly buyers. Their respective reactions thus will depend upon whether they are then performing primarily a consumption or a supply role.

To the extent that we can isolate the consumption effect, it would still appear that the demand for marijuana is quite inelastic in the ghetto or barrio.[9] It is certain that *moderate* increases in price or reduction in quality would have no visible effect on the overall demand. How much a *substantial* rise in prices or reduction in quality would affect consumer demand is considerably less certain. The fact is that the Watts youngsters already detect evidences of inflation in the marijuana market through declines in the quantity and quality of the product offered at the established prices. They feel that their need for it is so intense that they must accept and adjust to whatever changes have been detected on the street, but there is also some feeling that continued inflation could not realistically be tolerated. The following dialogue will illustrate these points:

*PB*: I was thinking about the irony that, maybe the marijuana economy seems to be more stable [i.e., less prone to drastic price movements], because years ago when I first began to learn some of the facts, a joint was fifty cents, and now for instance. . . .

*Willard*: Well, when they do sell it that way, it's fifty cents.

*PB*: Of course, you can have change in different ways and that is that you can maintain the same price of the item, but two things can happen—you can reduce the quantity of that item; like you sell a hamburger and a hamburger last year was fifty cents—you still have a fifty cent hamburger this year, but the patty will be smaller. The other thing is the quality of the item. For marijuana, this is the main question. But has the quality generally [changed] gone down over time, particularly over the last couple of years?

*Willard*: Well, it's really hard to say, because some is better than others.

*PB*: But this has always been true, right? I mean this was true two years ago.

*Willard*: Well, the quality of it—there is the difference right there. But the *quantity* of it—that's where it's bad. Because it used to be larger. That's the true difference between the last couple of years. The difference is the quantity, because it's a lot skimpier.

*PB*: You mean you get less for fifty cents?

*Willard*: Yes, for the bag, you know, you can buy a $5 bag where. . . .

*PB*: Is the bag supposed to contain so many ounces?

*Willard*: Yeah.

*PB*: Do you know how many ounces?

*Willard*: No, because it varies. Like, some cats, now when they sell it, if they don't have no means or measures, they just go by what they think it is, you know.

*PB*: If they think it's worth $5?

*Willard*: Right. Now, see, I know the change in quantity. . . . Now you can see that their outlook on the bag is there has to be a change because you are not getting what you used to get. You can tell. Okay, a couple of years back you might buy this special quantity to you and you know that . . . it would be twice the size that you buy today. And a couple of years ago—that's why I know the quantity or something has to be happening to slow this process . . . you know, to make an income. You know, there's not as much marijuana coming in as there was a couple of years ago.

*PB*: So you really have that kind of inflation there, too.

*Willard*: As a matter of fact, there was one time, I think last year, when you couldn't hardly find any, when you couldn't even find any.

*PB*: That was when they were trying to close the border . . .

*Willard*: Yeah, and they was burning up a lot of warehouses. It's like every other year when they beginning to have the elections. It was during election time.

*PB*: Any election, it gets scarcer?

*Willard*: I don't know what causes it, but it happens every year.

*PB*: . . . But let me get back to one point and that is the fact that prices themselves, like a "bag," a "lid"—are you saying that the prices haven't changed all that much?

*Willard*: Just the quality and the quantity.

*PB*: Just as a matter of general observation, do you think a consumer would buy less or does buy less?

*Willard*: In most cases, they don't really have a choice. If they really want to smoke—so they think—it's good and bad sometimes. See, they like marijuana, just like people like alcohol, you know. They just didn't change all of a sudden—they know how the times is, right now. They can see why the people—why the pushers are selling marijuana like this because they know and the people know that buy it from them, it's pretty skimpy now.

*Charles*: But you know one thing, there's one (thing) they have got to realize. See, a lot of people might get tired of that, because this is getting into $5 which is pretty hard to get.

*Willard*: Yeah and that's another thing. They have been going for it, see, they have been going for that quantity (which) is a lot smaller than it used to be; they have been going for it so far, but pretty soon it's going to have to open up. . . . Everybody knows about this unemployment crisis we have and the money like $5, for something that you knew you could get more of when you first started, plus the money is getting hard anyway.

Though the demand for pills apparently is more elastic and its magnitude limited in comparison with the market for marijuana, it still remains substantial in general economic terms.[10] In East Los Angeles, as well as Watts, "reds" are usually sold by the roll, containing four pills, at $1.00 per roll. The cost of "whites," or amphetamines, is $1.00 for a roll of ten. While some youngsters fear contamination of pills by amateur chemists, it appears that most of the pills are distributed in essentially the same form as they display when they emerge from the laboratories which produce them. The extent of the drug industry profit from these illicit markets is discussed later in this chapter.

Again taking their words at face value, the young people interviewed report that they are not as dependent upon pills as they obviously are upon "weed," and thus their demand presumably would be more affected by increases in price. It would also seem that the demand for "reds" or "whites" can be closely linked with the availability of marijuana, in the sense that a sharp limitation on the supply of "weed" might induce more youngsters to turn to pills as the most readily available, albeit highly imperfect, alternative. As a rule, they regard the effects of "grass" smoking as more pleasurable and safer than those obtained from the consumption of pills.

The supply of marijuana and pills, of course, is subject to the constraints imposed by its illegality, its dependence in some cases upon foreign sources, and the whims of politics and law enforcement. Some of the interviewees have noted a few of the cyclical patterns in the availability of marijuana, though most fluctuations are not so predictable. Clearly the decisions, often politically inspired, of federal and local officials and law enforcement officers have a recognizable impact on the ease with which the demand for illegal merchandise is met. Even foreign relations have a not inconsiderable effect, as much in the case of heroin, opium, and the other hard drugs as in the case of marijuana. Much of the supply of drugs and narcotics comes from Turkey, Mexico or the Orient, though some of it is home grown or manufactured and there is reason to believe that American firms are the major suppliers of the illegal pill market, knowingly or unknowingly.

The youngsters regard the market for marijuana as virtually limitless, suggesting thereby that it can perhaps absorb any forseeable increases in the supply. This is undoubtedly an exaggerated perception, and certainly at some point the expansion in supply would tend to push down prices, and possibly profits. We must take note of the fact, however, that a substantial market for marijuana now exists outside the ghettos and barrios, which may or may not absorb added supplies without reductions in unit price. Another imponderable, of course, is the future legal status of marijuana consumption and the extent to which legalization would strengthen both the demand and the supply. The interviewees observe cycles in the supply of marijuana, which they consistently attribute to politics and to politically inspired law enforcement changes, as in the following dialogue:

> *PB*: Do you think if the police wanted to control the distribution of marijuana, they could?
>
> *Willard*: Not necessarily. It would depend upon how they go about doing it, and if they had the right information.
>
> *PB*: I was saying earlier about the police on the take in New York City and what you're saying is that it's a big business. And it goes on, literally, under the noses of the people and the police. Do you think that the police ignore it because they really don't know what's going on? Or that they know what is going on but don't care? And when they do bust somebody, why does that particular person get busted and the big dealers never get busted?
>
> *Charles*: In the first place, the police is just like organized crime. . . . Now, this is my own personal feeling, I feel like this: I believe they let it slide—they know what's going on. They may not have it right on the pin head, not exactly, but they got a pretty good picture of what's happening. I feel that they let it happen like this because, actually, the people are asleep. . . . They're not aware of the fact that somebody has to supply this; they have to supply this. . . . Organized crime is just one small dot, just one small dot that has something to do with narcotics coming in. I'll tell you, I believe that the "establishment" is quite aware of this. . . .
>
> You know, who gives a damn? Like they say, it's down in the ghetto. As long as they're down in Inglewood sitting on some Champale—whatever they are doing, they don't give a damn until they find out that *their* daughter been tripping off of weed or whatever. Now, if it's their daughter, "I'm mad, now—they'll have to stop this shit. We have to bring this shit to the hole." Until about two years ago I believe that the shit was put on a stick like that. . . .
>
> *Robert*: I remember that—it was dry. For two months straight. I remember you could ride from where I live way out to the west side, on the other side of Los Angeles—way out to the west side, and couldn't find nothing.
>
> *Charles*: Yes. Right along that time. It was a really big thing. But then later, about six months later, they closed again, but you see, then traffic didn't slow up because organized crime, they thought of another means of getting it in. They just took Mexico off the map, you know. It wouldn't make that much difference, not now. People got too much

money invested—they couldn't let their money fall like that. Would you? Just because they were closing Mexico all of a sudden—just cry and sit while they bust you so you couldn't get over there—would you let that stop you? Could that stop you? You spend money to try to find out how to make more money. . . .

## The Risks

The youngsters view the trade in marijuana and pills as a "business," with both profits and risks. The risks, as noted, are not evenly distributed. The bigger dealers rarely are caught, while the teenager or young adult on the street will frequently accumulate a record for possession (usually simple possession, rather than possession for purposes of sale). On the other hand, the actual judicial penalties for first-offense possession normally are light: probation, a fine, and occasionally a short spell in jail. By and large only the youngster with a record of repeated offenses (both narcotics and other), or one who has antagonized local cops, will actually be imprisoned. Hence the legal penalties can be regarded as a form of business license tax. The worst effect, of course, is the presence of a narcotics record when the offender applies for future employment, the long-run consequences of which are discussed later in this study.

When dealing, the youngsters regard it as a relatively safe business as long as they keep a level head. Asked how many of the regular dealers would be picked up by the police, they replied:

> *Robert*: It's just one of those rare cases. Well, it's not really that much. You don't really hear if someone pops—if somebody drops a dime [informs].
> *Charles*: Only if they got busted on the humbug [accident or caprice]—yeah, they were high while trying to take care of business. You see, the world of dealing or transmission of drugs around in the community is just like having a job right here in Westwood. You don't come to work intoxicated unless you know that there are certain things that don't require you to use your brain; it's the same instance. This cat has an office, his office is the community.
> *Willard*: You keep a clean head.
> *Charles*: Right, your thinking ability has to be 100 percent

all the time because if you don't, you look behind you and there will be a big white man in a blue uniform. One thing: all they have to do is really satisfy the customer. That's right, 'cause that's like, you know, you got to be on your job satisfying the customers.[11]

The probability of getting caught, they believe, is in direct proportion to the number of others who are associated with the street dealer or are cognizant of his activities. The more one can deal independently and in relative secrecy, the less the likelihood that punishment will ensue. One young man stressed on several occasions that it is highly desirable *not* to have wives, girl friends, or others knowledgeable about one's street business; presumably such knowledge might endanger the dealer in the event of a quarrel or dispute, where motives of revenge or recrimination might lead to a police tipoff:

> *Willard*: The majority's [the big operators] not getting caught. Well, not too long ago one got picked up, but that was 'cause of him and his wife, or whatever, had a misunderstanding. And she turned him in. But the police didn't actually catch him.
>
> *Charles*: She put the nickel on him. But, see, like he more or less is the type of person where if he keeps a clear thinking mind and, like they say, pay your dues—you know, you been in a racket a little while, you know what you're doing, you know. If your hangup is gonna be a female—this is my personal opinion—I feel that she shouldn't have anything to do with it.
>
> *Willard*: So many of them got so many front men.
>
> *Charles*: You see, anything you do that deals with narcotics goes right back to your risk. Anything that's illegal goes back to your risk. You can be hung up by your front man, you can be hung up by your associates—people that come to take care of business with you. Don't try to play games with the big operators. This is what he's gonna tell you. "The bag not gonna get any fatter, you know. You just have to buy this to be cool. Don't come back to my pad if you don't dig it, you know?" Fronting him off like that, you know, shit. He'll blow your shit up just as fast and then he'll get you in a lot of trouble with the law and then get you in trouble with

the big man. You get hurt—it's not just a little nickel and dime thing—it's *thousands* of *dollars*.

*Willard*: Most of them that's in there—some of them might be doing it on their own, but not the majority—I mean they are doing it for somebody else.

There is always a risk that the police will detect one's supply and confiscate it, thereby wiping out the considerable investment which it represents. The perception is that this is very rare, however, and that individual policemen will be tolerant as long as the youngster is willing to share some of the "good stuff". These perceptions are absolutely consistent in both east Los Angeles and Watts, and even the wording is similar although the interviews were conducted separately and there was no opportunity for exchange of views or information between the two areas surveyed.

Watts:
    *Robert*: The police gets high, yeah! All of them get high.
    *Charles*: You know, the police, the establishment, they are the ones with the best weed, right, they got the good stuff.

East Los Angeles:
    *Pete*: There's this one cop that everyone knows that if he catches you under the influence he'll let you slide twice, if you behave yourself, and like there was once a couple of brothers were walking down the street and they had a case [of liquor] and instead of busting them they took the case and said, "You better not do that again." Usually they pour it out, or throw it away or something, but this case they just got it; it was an Anglo and a Chicano. They didn't bust us, they just took one of the cases away from us. I've known a lot that take advantage of you, that I know of. They don't hassle you; if you're loaded, you know, you got pills or something, as long as you give them, it's okay. He says, "How much you got?" or "What do you have in there?" you know, and then he says, "Well, give it to me." You know it's really weird, man.
    *PB*: That's interesting because in Watts they say the police have the best stuff or can get the best stuff.
    *Alfredo*: They do. They get the best stuff away from you. The dirty rats.

*Juan*: The pigs don't bust you if you have just one joint, they can't use that.

*Pete*: By the time you go to court, you know, they're through with it, you know, so they've got to get five joints out of you.

*Jose*: Well, they'll take it away from you and they'll let you go.

*Juan*: Even if you have two joints, they'll take one and say, "You better go home and if I see you around here again, I'll take you in." It's what happens.

The views expressed above, in both areas, are partly cause and partly effect of a virtually universal cynicism about the morals of the "moralists"—the policemen, public officials, and others identified with law and order. "It ain't nothing but a racket, just a racket, so far as the political structure is concerned. J. Paul Getty and Howard Hughes are going to do what they want to do, I don't care what the law is. A main function of the political structure is carried out through the police department. Did you notice what they campaigned on last time? Crime. They can get you any time they want to, but if they don't want to, like with Howard Hughes, they'll never get you. Now these peckerwoods get up there and run for President and say, 'Well, look, we want the police to enforce this, we want to enforce that,' it's just a racket, man."[12]

In any case, there is nothing to indicate that the existing legal penalties or enforcement of law provide any major deterrent to the functioning of the street economy. In general, the young people believe that the police and the courts will be reasonably lenient with them as long as they are concentrating on marijuana and staying away from drugs, especially hard drugs.

*Robert*: I say you can go to jail quicker for possession of drugs.

*Charles*: On a marijuana beef, man, you can get a little slack on that, man, the establishment goes easier. Where you have a case of marijuana, you know, when you go in there, you know they get on statistics, they lay it on your background. Yeah, check out your record, if you have been busted before, you been busted for drugs, you know what I mean, heroin, cocaine, mescalin, all that strong stuff, man. In the United States you come in and get busted for a $5 bag, man, cat gonna shoot some shit on you.

Even in cases of stealing, some youngsters feel strongly that survival demands it and the risks are worthwhile. Not even the possibility of a jail sentence frightens or deters them, and when a white is the victim, there is the added feeling that justice has been done, as the following dialogue among Watts youngsters will illustrate:

*Eddie*: We went into this shop. They had everything and a lady's purse sitting right there. We got the purse and left.

*Robert*: Oh, man—was she black or white?

*Eddie*: White.

*Jim*: Right on. Power to the people.

*Robert*: At this time, was you employed anywhere?

*Eddie*: No, I wasn't employed anywhere.

*Robert*: Okay, well, did you really have to have it?

*Eddie*: Yeah, I had to have it. At the time, yeah. We needed it. I needed it.

*Jim*: Need it at home or by yourself?

*Eddie*: At the home and for myself and for the sake of living, period.

*Jim*: Survival, right?

*Charles*: In other words, it's what you knew you had to do with it.

*Robert*: Now to me, in my own opinion and I think that J— and M— feel the same way, you know that was a good enough reason if any to risk going to jail for, 'cuz you will get fed in jail. You will reach your goal one way or another. And when you say about the pad, man, I know. Boy, when you're hungry that's the worst thing—that is sick. When you go to the pad and there ain't nothing in there.

Or, as another youngster summarized the feelings in a separate session: "Any kind of way a cat's gonna make it, be a risk, always a risk."

## Possible Effects of Legalization of Marijuana

It is obvious that the market for marijuana, in particular, has all of the characteristics of a regular consumer market (or what might be called, with great irony, the "white" market). It is based on an existing demand, has a price and marketing structure, and allocates resources in accordance with the principle of "consumer sovereignty." Only the fact that it is illegal distinguishes it from, say, the liquor or automobile or cosmetics markets. Logically, one would expect that the orthodox economists, who normally deplore governmental interferences with free-functioning markets and consumer sovereignty, would be in the forefront of those calling for legalization of the sale and purchase of marijuana.

It is possible, of course, that the production and sale of marijuana might entail certain external diseconomies which would lead to reductions in net output overall, though this opens up a Pandora's box from the viewpoint of the orthodox economists and therefore is a consideration which they tend to minimize or shun. A full exploration of the available findings on the effects of marijuana is beyond our scope here, but it now appears that the observable short-run or immediate consequences of its use are no more harmful, or perhaps less harmful, than those arising from the consumption of alcohol or tobacco. Whether there is a long-range physical or psychological disability associated with its continuous use is still uncertain, but there is as yet no scientifically verifiable evidence to support this fear. The fundamental reason for its present legal status, it would seem, is the Puritan ethic which denigrates the seeking of pleasure and exalts work and asceticism (an ethic which, at various times in our history, has produced legal restrictions on drinking, smoking, dancing, horse racing, theatrical performances, music, and myriad other forms of enjoyment).

As a personal aside, a kind of mystique has developed in connection with the use of marijuana, sometimes ascribing to it qualities and effects which I question. At best, I would not regard its effects as "superior" in any way to alcohol (as some of its more enthusiastic admirers proclaim), but this is a subjective opinion which is irrelevant to the matter of its legality. My impression is that, in accordance with some recent findings, its effect varies in line with the personality of the user and his predisposition as to the kind of response he wants and expects.

The young people recognize the glaring inconsistencies within the structure of our society and are united in their belief that the use of marijuana should be legalized. However, our discussions of the possible *economic* impact of this move raised questions in their minds which markedly lowered their enthusiasm for it. Apparently they have assumed that legalization would simply mean that they would secure it in the same way and same form as now, but that they would then suffer no legal penalties for its use. As they became aware that certain basic marketing and economic changes would take place as a result of legalization, they had second thoughts. Clearly, the legal sale of marijuana would be subject to licensing and other restrictions, taxation, and, probably, stronger or better enforced penalties than now exist for *un*lawful manufacture and distribution. Like the market changes which accompanied the repeal of the prohibition laws in 1933, these would have a profound impact on what is currently the subeconomy. The fears expressed by some of the Watts youngsters seem to take two forms: a belief that marijuana would be heavily taxed (which might raise the retail price) and otherwise regulated in a strict form which would take the advantage from their hands and give it to others; and an apprehension that it would lead to the destruction of their major source of income without the substitution of any alternative source.

> *George*: I believe marijuana would be legal right now if it was left up to the people. If everything was originally left up to the people, like the Bill of Rights, 'cuz the people are supposed to make the laws.
> *PB*: What do you think it's going to do to the market?
> *Robert*: You mean where's the money going to? They going to take all the goodies out of it! Would tax it, take all the goodies out of the shit! Better leave it like it is. That's a consideration.
> *Charles*: They would charge much, much more money for it.
> *Willard*: They would charge a little bit more money for it. They will tax the hell out of it. If you legalize marijuana it's gonna go up.

Some of their second thoughts about legalization stem from their cynicism and suspicion about the role of the establishment. As elsewhere, many are convinced that even more of the profits would leave the community if the marijuana trade became a legal business, subject to taxation and other regulation, and that the imposition of taxes might strengthen the motivation of government to penalize and eliminate its unlawful distribution on the streets.

> *Robert*: Man, I'd rather the shit stay just like it is. Uncle Sam, he won't be cool, he's the one that's going to have all the weed.

In principle, however, they think the consumption of marajuana should be legal:

> *Charles*: Right. I think they should go ahead and legalize weed and everybody get high and be happy.
> *George*: It would be a lot of chaos on that although I would like to see it legalized, because it's better to legalize it so when you do it you don't risk a chance.
> *Charles*: I look at it just like alcohol. If you wanna drink and wanna get high, that's up to you. But then if anything happens to you, you just go to the hospital, that's all.

Other comments suggest that many people would probably attempt to grow their own supply (untaxed) if marijuana usage became legal, but they also seem to agree that Uncle Sam would make a serious and effective attempt to control illegal manufacture, just as the legalization of alcohol led to the systematic decline and eventual destruction of bootlegging. As to whether legalization would lead to significant increases in demand, they believe that existing laws do have a preventive effect and that more people would smoke marijuana if it were legalized. A close examination of their reasoning, however, indicates that potential increases in demand would be concentrated in areas outside the ghetto and barrio and perhaps among the older age groups. It is not at all certain that young men in the central city *could* expand their consumption substantially, and if the overall economic effects of legalization diminish or undermine their present role in the sub-economy, it is possible that they might then be unable to afford as much.

If either legalization or law enforcement does, in fact, have these consequences, the economic crisis in the ghettos and barrios, already of disastrous proportions, would intensify to the point of social chaos *unless* provisions are made for replacement of the lost income through other channels. As suggested elsewhere, the relative peace in inner-city areas during periods of severe economic recessions is probably due, in large part, to the stabilizing influence of the subeconomy and the interest of its major operators in preventing violent interruptions of normal business.

There are groups, of course, which believe that the drug trade is intentionally encouraged or promoted by the "establishment" as a means of tranquilizing ghetto residents and preventing them from carrying through plans for radical and perhaps revolutionary reforms. The Black Muslims, as one example, deplore the widespread use of marijuana and other drugs, and see this as a reflection of deliberate outside control over the ghetto. Whether or not one accepts this Machiavellian interpretation literally, it is undeniable (as the next chapter demonstrates in detail) that the majority group has traditionally tolerated the pervasive use of pills, narcotics, and other illegal items or services as long as it was believed to be confined to low-income ghetto communities.

## Effect on Work Attitudes

The availability of an illegal income naturally affects the willingness of young people to accept legal employment at wages below the level attainable in the subeconomy. Though this fact enrages Professor Banfield and other exponents of Social Darwinism and the Puritan ethic, it is entirely consistent with the premises and precepts of competitive economics. Since the subeconomy is actually a form of consumer market, it is economically appropriate for the worker to offer his services at the higher income level associated with that market rather than to accept lower wages in the types of work considered morally superior by Banfield and others. The orthodox economists, of course, should be willing to pursue the logic of the doctrine of consumer sovereignty wherever it might lead, without making the value judgments which in other contexts they deplore so articulately.

Manifestly, these facts also render irrelevant much of the controversy over the presumed impact of minimum wages upon employment.[13] Thousands of young men already express no interest in unskilled jobs paying the full minimum wage and above. Professor Doeringer's concept of the dual queue—reciprocal rankings by job-seekers and employers—helps explain why many young men, quite logically from their viewpoint, reject low-paying jobs (particularly those involving manual labor). They rank preferred employers just as the employers rank preferred workers, and accept the less preferred alternatives only when the better ones are no longer available. Again, what is sauce for the middle-class goose should be sauce for the inner-city gander.

> *PB*: Back to the economics of the situation. At most from an NYC job you can make maybe $1.45 to $1.65 an hour. A training program has an allowance which is maybe $60 a week. In your opinion, is this an important reason why a lot of people who might be eligible for a training program or eligible for NYC may not even be interested in going in that direction?
> *Charles*: You can't compare them.
> *Willard*: Right. 'Cuz they're making money.

These impressions and observations are consistent with the available statistics on employment in many of the special governmental programs and in low-paid jobs in private industry. Between the initiation of the Neighborhood Youth Corps program in fiscal 1965 to the end of fiscal 1970, approximately 318,000 enrollment slots went unfilled. From fiscal 1964 through fiscal 1970 almost 147,000 MDTA (Manpower Development and Training Act) slots similarly went begging. This same pattern holds true for a number of other programs supposedly intended to increase employment and employability for residents of low-income areas, including young men (and in the case of NYC, young persons exclusively).[14]

The official statistics on numbers of "discouraged workers" are also impressive. The number of such workers, often labeled "the hidden unemployed," rose approximately 125,000 to a total of 740,000 (seasonally adjusted) between the second quarter of 1970 and the corresponding quarter of 1971. Most of the men falling in this category were either under 25 or over 60, thus indicating that a substantial percentage will be found in the age group studied in this report. This Bureau of Labor Statistics study reports that Blacks tend to be even more overrepresented among discouraged workers than among those regularly counted as unemployed (and thus in the labor market). It speculates that we probably do not know all the real reasons why such large numbers do not enter, or leave, the labor force.[15] Some of the underlying reasons may perhaps be suggested in our analysis of the youth labor market and the subeconomy in Los Angeles. It should again be noted that official statistics usually *under*state the magnitude of this problem.

Young men in the central city, for a number of reasons, will often tend to set a "reservation wage" for their acceptance of proffered employment which exceeds the actual wage established. Thus whatever effect a reduction in wages would have upon *demand* (and even that is uncertain, given the reluctance of many employers to hire unskilled minority youngsters under any circumstances), it would even further discourage the *supply* of young people for such work. Professor Banfield, as noted earlier, is aware of this fact and deplores it. It may, indeed, have deleterious long-run consequences, but it hardly seems sensible to blame the young men who are responding logically *to those alternatives which society has made available to them.*

## The Profits of "Sin"

One of the critical reasons why the subeconomy is tolerated is that it is highly profitable to important sectors of the regular economy. Society has deemed the preservation of the subeconomy preferable to the establishment of family income guarantees at a level above the poverty line, or the reform of existing employment structures to accommodate the needs of those excluded rather than of those included. It has been cheaper and simpler to permit the subeconomy to function, producing some income for ghetto and barrio residents as a pacifier. This alternative is rendered even more attractive by the fact that a significant part of the revenue flows into the coffers of legitimate businesses, usually controlled by Anglos.

Though much of this process is hidden from view, enough visible evidence remains to confirm the above observation. The actual cost of producing a "red" (Seconal capsule, known as a "downer") is from one half to one cent each. Thus at the retail street price of twenty-five cents per pill, the profits have multiplied 25 or 50 times the actual manufacturing cost. According to estimates of experts, from a quarter to a half of the annual production of barbituates is diverted to illegal uses and 92 percent of "up and down" pills in illicit traffic are manufactured by legitimate drug companies; whatever estimate is accepted, it is clear that a large percentage of pill production in this country finds its way into the subeconomy. Senator Gaylord Nelson of Wisconsin, who has investigated the drug industry, has stated that pet food factories are inspected more frequently than are those producing prescription drugs. The issue of *Congressional Quarterly* for December 4, 1970, contains a special report on the successful lobbying by the Swiss-based drug manufacturing firm of Hoffman-LaRoche against government regulation of its top selling tranquilizer drugs, and adds that amphetamine ("uppers") producers also won lobbying victories despite reports that much of their production was going into the "black market."[16] In 1967 the Federal Trade Commission revealed that the U.S. drug industry had *the highest profits of any industry group in the country*. The drug manufacturers averaged 21.1 percent profit on investment—*after* taxes.[17]

Further information provided in the June 24, 1971 issue of *Standard and Poor's Industry Surveys* reveals that ethical drug industry profits in 1971 were then expected to rise 10 percent to a total of about $7.7 billion, and that the "demand for drug products is generally recession resistant, and the return on sales is among the best in U.S. industry." Furthermore, this growth will accelerate: "Sales by the ethical drug industry are expected to rise to approximately $10.8 billion in 1975 and to $15.4 billion by 1980."[18] This means a growth rate of 8-9 percent annually. It is also reported that most of the major drug companies have established tax-exempt operations in Puerto Rico.

Though outside the scope of our discussion here, the profits realized by organized crime through the sale of hard narcotics are staggering. More immediately relevant are the proceeds from the sale of marijuana, which flow again into "respectable" coffers. Much of this has already been documented. Perhaps a more dramatic illustration appeared in a news item in the *Los Angeles Times* of December 16, 1971:

> Something new on the drug scene was seized Wednesday when officers raided what they described as a major narcotics and dangerous drugs "factory" *in a plush home in Laguna Beach.*

Among materials seized was a gallon of hashish oil, described as something police had not previously seen.

It is 40 to 50 times more powerful than high grade hashish, and one drop on the end of a cigarette can give a person a "high."

Police said they also seized 30,000 LSD tablets, 5 ounces of high grade cocaine and 8 pounds of marijuana, some canned and sealed for shipment. The contraband was valued at $150,000. [Emphasis added.]

The discouraging aspect of this news item is that it appears so rarely. This is no accident, however. The subeconomy, with its usual effect on the ghettos, has been a permanent and traditional feature of American society, partly because it has been so convenient and so profitable to the majority group. The next chapter documents this generalization through an exploration of history.

NOTES

1. *U. S. News and World Report*, December 7, 1970, p. 44, citing figures reported by the House Select Committee on Crime and the Bureau of Narcotics and Dangerous drugs.

2. *Ibid.*, p. 44.

3. *Ibid.*, p. 43.

4. Peter Doeringer, "Manpower Programs for Ghetto Labor Markets," Proceedings of the 21st Annual Winter Meeting, Industrial Relations Research Association, December 29-30, 1968, pp. 263-264.

5. Bruno Stein, *On Relief: The Economics of Poverty and Public Welfare*, New York: Basic Books,, 1971, pp. 96, 98.

6. *Manpower Report of the President, 1971*, pp. 98-99, citing a study by Stanley Friedlander of the Conservation of Human Resources Staff, Columbia University.

7. This appears to be a slip of the tongue or a miscalculation, because the current street price for "reds" is 25¢ a pill, or $1.00 for a roll of *four* pills. Thus there should have been 12 "reds" in three rolls, though perhaps the market for pills in Watts was somewhat different at that particular time.

8. The last sentence of this paragraph, as published in a local news article, caused the Police Commission of Los Angeles to issue a subpoena requiring the appearance of the author at a public hearing, in March 1972, on the strange grounds that the sentence in question implies my possession of unrevealed, private evidence of corruption within the Los Angeles Police Department. Obviously, it is not directed exclusively at any one law enforcement agency, or for that matter any other specific political or legal agency in Los Angeles alone, but the voluminous documentation supporting this generalization may be found in the following chapter.

9. Professors Charles T. Nisbet and Firouz Vakil of UCLA recently sampled a number of UCLA students on questions related to their usage of marijuana and its economic effects. Basic differences in samples make it impossible to compare their results directly with our own. Apparently they

found that the demand for marijuana was somewhat more elastic than would probably be the case in Watts—a result which I would have expected.

10. As an informal indication of how profitable pill hustling can be, an adult man (now somewhat prominent in Los Angeles) once told me in private conversation that, some years ago when he was hustling in New York, he earned more than $20,000 a year from the sale of pills alone.

11. Compare these completely spontaneous comments with the following account of why Irishmen lost out to other ethnic groups in the rackets of New York, written by D. P. Moynihan: Addiction to alcohol "partially accounts for the disappearance of the Irish from organized crime. Gambling and related activities are among the largest business activities in New York and certainly among the most profitable. With their political power, even if declining, the Irish ought to have a share of control in them, but the Southern Italians, with Jewish connections, have completely taken over. Bookmaking, policy, and drugs are complex, serious, exacting trades. They are not jobs for heavy drinkers." *Beyond the Melting Pot,* by Nathan Glazer and D. P. Moynihan, Cambridge: MIT Press and Harvard University Press, 1963, p. 257.

12. *Watts: The Aftermath,* Paul Bullock (ed.), New York: Grove Press, 1970, p. 144.

13. This is not to suggest, of course, that the minimum wage necessarily has no impact on employment anywhere in the economy. This study is limited to those areas where the subeconomy is active and large numbers of workers rarely work at jobs covered by social security and other forms of social insurance, through which it may be possible to trace their employment pattern. Outside the low-income ghetto, it is conceivable that minimum-wage legislation does have a measurable employment impact, but this is not our concern here.

14. See p. 299 of the *Manpower Report of the President, 1971.* The *Wall Street Journal* of December 14, 1971 reports that only about half of the available slots under the new public service job law has been filled as of that date, far behind schedule and below expectations. The article attributes much of the difficulty to bureaucratic delays and resistance from employee organizations, but it may also reflect the reluctance of jurisdictions to offer anything but low level make-work, thus triggering some of the reactions already noted. See also Edwin Harwood, "Youth Unemployment—A Tale of Two Ghettos," *The Public Interest,* Fall 1969, pp. 78-87. Harwood notes that the out-of-school NYC program in Houston, Texas encountered many of these resistances.

15. *Daily Labor Report,* August 26, 1971, p. B-4.

16. *Congressional Quarterly,* December 4, 1970, p. 2911 ff. Those familiar with the New Deal of the 1930s will find a certain irony in the fact that the law firms representing the drug industry were those of Thomas G. (Tommy) Corcoran and (Thurman) Arnold and (Paul) Porter. See also *U. S. News and World Report,* December 7, 1970, p. 44.

17. Figures cited in Evelyn Dubrow, "Our Other Drug Problem," *Viewpoint,* Fall, 1971, p. 19.

18. *Standard & Poor's Industry Surveys,* June 24, 1971, pp. H13 and H14.

# 8

---

# THE SUBECONOMY IN AMERICAN HISTORY

In his definitive account of the prohibition era and the role of the bootlegger, Andrew Sinclair gives prominence to a quotation from Al Capone: "I make my money by supplying a public demand. If I break the law, my customers, who number hundreds of the best people in Chicago, are as guilty as I am. The only difference between us is that I sell and they buy. Everybody calls me a racketeer. I call myself a businessman. When I sell liquor, it's bootlegging. When my patrons serve it on a silver tray on Lake Shore Drive, it's hospitality."[1]

Capone's statement, however self-serving it may be, is an insightful commentary on the economic function of many law-breakers in the urban areas of the United States, then and now. The subeconomy is hardly a new phenomenon in American life, nor has it historically been limited to the Black and Brown ghettos. Sometimes it has functioned directly through political machines and public corruption, as in New York City and other large metropolitan areas in the nineteenth century and earlier in the twentieth century. On other occasions it has operated quasi-independently, but always with the implied or explicit cooperation of government and the law enforcement agencies. From the earlier concentration on graft and the operation of saloons, gambling houses and brothels (as in New Orleans' famous Storyville district), it progressed to the large-scale racketeering of the prohibition era from the end of World War I to 1933. With the passing of prohibition, the emphasis shifted again to illegal betting, gambling and, most notably, the supply of narcotics and drugs of all varieties.

Traditionally, much of the illegal economic activity has centered in low-income areas of the city, though the consumer market for the products of this activity often has covered the entire city. In the earlier periods the "immigrant" ghetto served as a major locus of the subeconomy and a source from which the lower-level criminals or corrupt entrepreneurs were commonly drawn. Significant proceeds from this activity, however, flowed outside the ghettos into the coffers of politicians, industrialists and other businessmen, union leaders, policemen, and others who might be generally regarded as "respectable."

There is apparently a high correlation between ethnicity and economic crime. In the nineteenth century the Irish gravitated to the big-city political machines, and displayed a taste for politics which enabled them to rise into the higher echelons by the end of the century. In 1880 New York's Tammany Hall elected the first Irish Catholic mayor, and this domination persisted for another half century. Daniel Patrick Moynihan, surely no enemy of the Irish, has commented that among the Irish "there was an indifference to Yankee proprieties. To the Irish, stealing an election was rascally, not to be approved, but neither quite to be abhorred."[2] The Irish, accustomed to official persecution because of their religion, tended to suspect law and formal government and to prefer informal political and social processes.

Of course, the early political machines performed social welfare functions for virtually all of the immigrant groups and for many of the indigenous poor. In return for their necessary political support, the poor and the recent arrivals were given public jobs, relief, Christmas and Thanksgiving baskets, and other favors. Such interference with the free market and "survival of the fittest" was, naturally, contrary to the most cherished doctrines of the laissez-faire economists and their potent allies in the conservative classes.

The disreputable role of the Irish, however, was not limited to the performance of these formally disapproved but socially useful functions. They became heavily involved in waterfront activities, on all sides, and corruption has been endemic to the waterfront economy even to the present day. "The Irish, in a sense, have never strayed far from the docks, where they established a singularly dispiriting regime of political, business, and trade union corruption."[3] In the twentieth century other minorities have gravitated to waterfront employment and its concomitant graft: first the Italians, and later the Blacks and Puerto Ricans.

The new immigration waves in the late nineteenth and early twentieth centuries brought the Italians from southern Europe and the Jews from eastern Europe. The newer immigrants again provided the human raw material for the subeconomies of the cities. Some of the immigrant Jewish economic success came through legitimate channels in merchandising, banking, and building, but many Jews concentrated in the garment industry where sweatshops were prevalent and racketeers not infrequently played a role in labor disputes. In the 1920s both the Jewish-led employer association and the Jewish-led union hired muscle men to serve them in industrial disputes, and both later discovered that all of the thugs were employed by the same man: Arnold Rothstein.[4]

The coming of prohibition boosted the subeconomy to a pinnacle of affluence. Again the ethnic minorities were the major risk-takers, and by the end of prohibition almost all of the prominent racketeers were Italian, Jewish or Irish. The southern Italians, notably the Sicilians, provided much of the manpower for operation of the bootlegging empires in cities like Chicago and New York, but the chief consumers of their illegal goods were the Anglo-Saxon whites. Of greatest interest, in terms of the main focus of this study, was the role of the low-income ghetto dweller in this massive operation. Young men in the poor sections of Chicago learned from experience that crime "is the only avenue available to them."[5] The bootlegger and racketeer was a hero in the poverty neighborhood, someone to be envied and emulated rather than despised. Sinclair describes the role and influence of the prohibition racketeer in terms which can be applied word for word to the subeconomy in Watts and east Los Angeles (substituting only "Black" or "Chicano" for "Sicilian" or "Italian"; "marijuana" or "pills" for "bootleg liquor"; and "Black Panthers" or "Brown Berets" for "Unione Siciliano") :

> The wealthy racketeer and bootlegger was, in the eyes of the Italian or the Slavic community, the American dream come true. The recent immigrants had come to America in pursuit of a golden mirage, and those among them who made fortunes by violating antipathetic laws were their first heroes and helpers. They were the "successes of the neighborhood." The prestige and power of the Unione Siciliano gave all poverty-stricken Sicilians a hope in the future and a certain national pride against an America which discriminated against them. Only those few Sicilians who had respectable jobs in middle-class professions hated the reputation which the Unione gave to the Sicilian people. The plea of such priests as Father Louis Giambastiani against the internecine slaughter of the Sicilian gangs was rare in a community which associated wealth and power with criminal action.
>
> The chief sources of bootleg liquor in all major cities by the close of prohibition were to be found in the tenements, in the Little Italys and Little Bohemias of the slums. There the tenement dwellers were organized by the gangsters into an army of alky cookers and booze runners. The accusation of the drys that most of the large bootleggers were of foreign extraction was correct; but the contentions of the wets that most of the hard liquor drinkers, who kept the bootleggers in business, were of old American stock were also correct. Indeed, the patronage of the new America by the old was one of the first efforts made by the old America to look after the welfare of the new. Although the prohibition laws only proceeded against the sellers and manufacturers of bootleg, not the buyers, with the consequence that the foreign-born landed in jail more frequently than their patrons, Americans of an older vintage were responsible for keeping the bootleg trade in such a healthy financial state. And even though a higher percentage of foreign-born Americans were sentenced for drunkenness and violation of liquor laws and neglect of their families, the virtue of the native-born could hardly be maintained on the basis of crime figures. For a higher percentage of native white Americans violated narcotics laws, and the laws against fraud, forgery, robbery, adultery and rape.[6]

Like the Irish before them, the Italians and Jews suffered crippling discrimination in the labor market and in American society generally, partly because of their religions and partly because harmful stereotypes gave rise to deeply rooted prejudices among the dominant Anglo whites. All minorities had been told, in effect, that their cultures and their religious beliefs were inferior to those held by the Anglo-Saxons. Quite apart from the usual prejudices based on religion, vicious canards were hurled at the poorer and often illiterate immigrants. The south Italian and Sicilian peasants were "considered inferior, hardly civilized."[7] The earliest southern Italian immigrants came from farming areas, and more than half of these immigrants over the age of 14 were illiterate (just as the Black immigrants to urban centers in the United States often emerge from rural communities in the South and also suffer severe educational deprivation). Skeptical toward law and government (like the Irish), with most of the better jobs barred to them because of discrimination and their educational deficiencies, the southern Italians replaced the Irish in unskilled jobs on railroad and construction projects or engaged in criminal enterprise. Glazer and Moynihan again note:

> Opportunities for wealth and prominence came slow and late to Italian Americans. Meanwhile, gambling, drugs, and the waterfront succeeded industrial racketeering and bootlegging as the major sources of illegal wealth. Into this field, as the older groups withdrew, the new group moved. By the time of the Kefauver investigations in the early 1950s, a large part of the gambling and other illegal industries had fallen almost completely into the hands of Italian Americans. And in their hands they apparently remain, because the Negroes and Puerto Ricans have not shown the ability to capture them.[8]

The early racketeers were poorly educated and young. At the height of his vast power, Al Capone was only 29 years old.[9] The farther they moved from the slums and the more wealthy they became, the greater became their social and economic respectability. Capone proudly consorted with celebrities and popular sports figures. Without strong political and police support, the criminal empires would soon have toppled; the administration of Chicago's Mayor "Big Bill" Thompson (whose fame mainly rests upon his politically inspired threat to punch England's King George on the nose, should he visit Chicago) openly tolerated and secretly connived with the racketeers, and the enforcement of prohibition laws at the federal level was characterized by a studied apathy and indifference. Prohibition had its strong supporters in the Midwest and the South and in rural communities and small towns generally, but in the cities the bootlegger was not without sympathy and respect. As long as the violence was largely confined to gang warfare and stayed away from the respectable neighborhoods, the wealthy and the middle class were prepared to accept racketeering as essential to the provision of their booze.

In the nineteenth century the linkage between crime and the local government had been direct and obvious, reflected in the power of the political machine. In the twentieth century the linkage was sometimes as overt as it had been earlier (as in the case of Chicago and Cicero in Illinois) but more often it tended to be somewhat indirect and concealed. Civil service reform and other events had diluted the strength of the traditional machines, but, nevertheless, politics and criminal enterprises continued their partnership. During the Depression, testimony before the Wickersham Commission clearly delineated the relationship between criminal activity and the political structure; Matthew Woll, a vice president of the American Federation of Labor, noted that there was no general feeling of resentment against the racketeers "because they are looked upon as being part of a trade to satisfy a social want," and that there was little attempt to enforce the law "even for the most vicious crime committed." Not one of the 130 gang murders in Chicago between 1926 and 1927 was punished legally.[10] Corruption was pervasive; only the particularly brutal St. Valentine's Day Massacre in 1929 finally sparked an effective public reaction against the racketeers and led to a tightening of law enforcement.

Bootlegging, of course, disappeared with the end of prohibition. Many of the bootleggers, especially at the higher levels, were jailed (Capone for income tax evasion) or fled the country, but others simply converted to lawful business enterprises or continued their illicit activity in other fields: organized gambling, racetrack betting, the numbers game, prostitution, and narcotics. In cities like New York the ethnic composition of the economic criminal group began to change somewhat, as more Blacks (and later the Puerto

Ricans) entered the lower echelons. By this time opportunities had opened up for Italian Americans in legitimate areas of economic activity and an Italian middle class, respectable and relatively conservative, had emerged. Nevertheless, the top leadership of the rackets tended to remain in the hands of the Italian Americans.

On the streets of the ghettos—in Harlem, Chicago's South Side, Philadelphia's Jungle, Central Avenue and Watts in Los Angeles, and elsewhere—the Blacks had entered the subeconomy in massive numbers, serving as the local "policy dealers" and drug peddlers. Like the Irish and the Jews and the Italians before them, they took the risks and, in return, claimed a part of the income generated by these activities. An important part of the income, of course, flowed into the hands of outsiders who controlled the operation at the top and arranged for the supply of pills, marijuana, and the hard dope like heroin and cocaine. The local police always took their share, as did politicians (sometimes through campaign contributions and other support from the "businessmen" who ran the rackets), some doctors and lawyers, and others in the complex network of crime.[11]

Originally the trade in marijuana and related drugs was largely confined to the ghettos. "Weed" became associated in the public mind with the poor Blacks, jazz musicians, and some entertainers. In the early 1930s, Cab Calloway sang about the "Reefer Man," and Louis Armstrong was once arrested by the Los Angeles police for smoking a "joint" in a parking lot next to the hall where he was playing, an event which apparently caused him to abandon the habit as being too risky to his career. Young Blacks, again like their ethnic predecessors, found that street crime was "the only avenue available to them." Marijuana and the harder drugs served both as sources of erratic income and means of temporary psychic escape from the tensions generated by prejudice, discrimination and slum ghetto living.

Although by the late 1930s the sale and use of marijuana had been made a crime under both federal and state laws, the enforcement of these laws became highly selective. Just as in the days of prohibition, when racketeering and violence aroused little indignation as long as they stayed within certain neighborhoods of the city and certain elements of the society, the use of narcotics and the playing of numbers hardly disturbed the general population as long as these crimes and *any violence or personal crime associated with them* were limited to the low-income minority areas.

Gambling and related forms of crime have not been restricted to the residents of ghettos; the illegal offtrack betting operations, as one example, have been largely patronized by the Anglos. Oscar Handlin finds no substantial evidence that Negroes and Puerto Ricans commit significantly more crime in New York City than previous immigrant minorities or the Anglos. There are, he observes, particular *types* of crime that are more characteristic of the ghettos and barrios, a fact which he ascribes primarily to certain cultural factors such as family disorganization and social attitudes:

> With reference to still other forms of delinquency, the incidence among Puerto Ricans and Negroes may not be significantly greater than in other segments of the population, but violations of the law are not regarded within the group with the moral disapprobation attached to them in the wider community. Neither the Negroes nor the Puerto Ricans see any ethical deficiencies in gambling; and they accept policy and its associated rackets as a matter of course. If the numbers is regarded as an evil at all, it is a necessary one that plays a useful part in the lives of men and women for whom advancement is more a dream than a possible reality. But the long history of gambling in the city and its prevalence among other groups show that what is different is the form and the open acceptance rather than the extent of participation.[12]

Cultural factors undeniably play an important role in explaining ethnic differences in types of criminal activity, but associated with and underlying these factors are powerful economic forces. As this historical review has demonstrated, society has tolerated and encouraged the ghetto subeconomies partly to meet consumer needs (in and out of the ghetto) usually regarded as immoral, and partly to provide an income to poverty groups under circumstances requiring no direct cost to the taxpayer and no entry by minorities into those parts of the labor market where they might compete with the majority group which currently dominates. As I shall elaborate later, this has had the added advantages of imposing the major risks upon the "unpopular" minorities while, at the same time, assuring that a not insignificant part of the economic gains flows back into the Anglo community, directly through the Anglo ownership of drug-producing firms, gambling establishments, etc., and indirectly through Anglo control of the stores and other businesses serving ghetto neighborhoods.

The economic and psychological effect of this arrangement upon the young man should be obvious. It reinforces his cynicism about law and order and creates the expectation that only through the subeconomy can he meet his economic needs. Clarence Williams III, actor and star of the television show "Mod Squad," recently described how he began his "career" as a policy runner in the New York ghetto. Every morning, he explained, he would stand in hallways and pick up the small numbers bets from older women, and would deliver the winnings at the end of the day to those who had scored a hit. The racket operators had an agreement with the local cops which normally protected the dealers, but Williams ultimately was arrested when temporary political pressure on the police department required that he be sacrificed. The bigger operators were not molested. In a recent book, a young cocaine dealer describes the fine art of police bribery:

> Uptown the other night we had a big dice game goin' on. First the uniformed cops came by in the car, and the players gave them five dollars apiece, ten dollars. Then an hour or so later another car comes by with a Black cop and a White cop and a sergeant. So they gave them twenty dollars—five dollars for each of the cops and ten dollars for the sergeant. Don't you know that twenty minutes later here comes two narco detectives. They gave them some money, I don't know just how much. Now, at this point, had any more cops come, it would have been a bitch out there, 'cause they had pushed it to the bust. They had really pushed it to the wire. Somebody would have said "fuck them cops" and they would have kept on playing. And then the cops would have got out the car because they didn't get no money, and they're maybe dumb enough to start hassling people. You hear how a cop gets stabbed, fight breaks out, ten people get arrested.
>
> Look, I can understand a uniformed cop looking for two dollars, five dollars out in the street. He's out there hustlin'. He wants to get some money to take home to his wife and kids, or whatever. Okay, they're money hungry because they're human. But do you know how much they take a week in bribes? Do you know that if there's five crap games, and

they come around every two hours and get ten dollars, five dollars apiece, all night long, and if they do that five days a week, do you know how much they're getting in graft?[13]

In what must be one of the most unique charges of discrimination ever made, then Congressman Adam Clayton Powell complained several years ago that the New York police in Harlem favored the Italian and Jewish policy bankers over the Black. Recent investigations by the Knapp Commission in New York, inquiries into police malpractices at the Hollywood detective division in Los Angeles, and other studies have produced evidence that many policemen are active partners in the subeconomy, and that their role in protecting and benefiting from it is more than just an accidental or occasional one. In a recent *Wall Street Journal* article, David S. Anderson of the *Journal* editorial staff cited a statement of Professor Bernard Cohen, a Queens College criminologist who has studied police misconduct in New York City, that "I don't think cops are any worse now than they always have been. I think much of this went on 30 and 40 years ago, but nobody said anything about it." Anderson cites several experts on criminology to support a conclusion that police corruption is not simply a matter of individual wrongdoing, but rather of systemic pressure. Further, the enforcement, at least in theory, of laws governing so-called victimless crimes breeds cynicism in many young policemen. "The moral confusion is in some ways inherent in laws the policemen must enforce, notably those against the so called victimless crimes of gambling, prostitution, and drug abuse. Though legally proscribed, these activities are flourishing businesses in many cities, businesses the policeman and his neighbors might even feel inclined to patronize from time to time." Stanford law professor Herbert Packer is quoted as saying that "as long as we have laws like that, police are going to be corrupt."[14]

Professor Albert Reiss, Jr., of Yale University, whose definitive study of police practices in three major cities (Boston, Chicago, and Washington, D.C.) has recently been published, remarks that: "The policing of vice erodes police authority when police impose a standard that is unpopular with a substantial segment of the local community. Selective enforcement of unpopular laws invariably is seen as the arbitrary exercise of authority. The policing of vice also tends to undermine police authority because it leaves police vulnerable to subversion through the corruption of police conduct; a corrupt police can hardly lay claim to legitimacy of moral authority."[15]

Reiss' researchers found that approximately one out of every five policemen in the three cities studied committed criminal violations of law *while under observation*, or admitted to researchers that they had thus trespassed. This *excludes* any participation in syndicated crime, or violations of departmental regulations such as the acceptance of favors and gratuities from local businessmen. The study team ascertained that about one third of the merchants and small businessmen in high-crime areas openly acknowledged such favors. Reiss observes that the noncriminal violations sometimes represent a relatively harmless and voluntary payment by businessmen for special, legitimate services rendered by policemen.

Many of the criminal violations admitted by policemen or committed under observation were connected with the subeconomy or themselves constituted a kind of subeconomy (for instance, the accepting of bribes from deviants or traffic offenders; the taking of merchandise from a burglarized establishment). Reiss comments that "the bulk of offenses committed by officers provide income supplements derived from exchange relationships."[16] It must again be emphasized that most of these criminal acts by policemen took place under observation, and that the officers *knew* they were being observed. Common sense alone suggests the probability that many more such actions will occur when the policeman is not under observation.

Ramsey Clark, former Attorney General of the United States, notes that in 1968, shortly after the merger of the Bureau of Narcotics and the Bureau of Drug Abuse Control into the Department of Justice, "more than fifty agents were discharged and over a dozen indicted for selling narcotics or accepting bribes."[17] Clark's observations exactly parallel those of Professor Reiss:

The police are widely exposed to temptations of bribery by their inadequate salaries and lack of professional competence and pride. Why should an underpaid officer moonlight four hours a day when he can make as much by ignoring a bookmaking operation that seems impossible to stop anyway? What's the harm? Slowly the rackets buy protection, corrupting a sergeant or a lieutenant, several patrolmen, a court clerk or magistrate, an assistant district attorney, a deputy warden or probation officer. The major restraints on organized crime ultimately become the self-discipline of the bosses, who do not want to risk a public outcry, and the limited purchasing power of the poor.

As long as we satisfy some vague moral need by outlawing conduct we cannot control, and while we care so little that we crowd poor and powerless people into violent slums, and while through neglect we rely on underpaid and undertrained police for law enforcement, we will have organized crime in many forms and a steady supply of illegal goods and services to the poor. This should surprise no one.[18]

On March 22, 1972, a former Los Angeles police intelligence officer was sentenced to 25 years in federal prison for narcotics traffic, after federal narcotics agents had found $320,000 worth of cocaine in his home. The officer left the police force after his arrest. It hardly needs emphasizing that one member of the police *intelligence* division must be worth scores of patrolmen to the denizens of organized crime and the higher echelons of the subeconomy.

Perhaps the bluntest statement has recently been made by a former deputy police commissioner of the city of New York: "Indeed, it may be stated as an axiom that no illegal activity which is dependent on a sizable retail trade can operate in any city without the cooperation of crooked cops."[19]

The American Bar Association's Special Committee on Crime Prevention and Control, headed by attorney Edward Bennett Williams and containing representatives of law enforcement and the judicial system as well as academicians, has condemned the "overcriminalization" reflected in laws applying criminal sanctions to victimless acts. Arguing that these laws lead to "a significant drain on the resources of our criminal justice system," the Committee calls for repeal and the substitution of noncriminal methods and procedures for the handling of legitimate medical or social problems.[20] For our purposes, the Committee's comments on the effect of such laws are especially relevant:

Enforcement of gambling and prostitution laws does more than unnecessarily drain criminal justice resources. It also tends to corrupt the enforcer. The New York City Commission to Investigate Alleged Police Corruption has identified gambling and prostitution as two of the principal sources of police corruption. Gambling and prostitution are commercial enterprises, frequently controlled by crime syndicates. They yield high profits, and the payoff is simply a necessary cost of business. The prostitute who works the streets can stay in business only as long as the policeman on the beat looks the other way. Frequently he will be paid by the girl or her procurer to look the other way.

The Committee cites estimates placing payoffs from numbers operators in New York City at a figure of $15 million yearly. While conceding that most policemen are honest, the report contends that the money available from the subeconomy is an unnecessary source of temptation for those who are corruptible. "Their willingness to accept that money can perhaps be explained in part by the futility of trying to eliminate prostitution and gambling through the criminal sanction. Prostitution and gambling are as old as mankind, and prostitutes and gamblers will continue to exist as long as there is a demand for their services."[21]

Another harmful effect of laws against victimless crime, as noted by the ABA committee, is the practice of selective law enforcement under which the policeman himself decides whether and in what manner to enforce. "Selective law enforcement is a highly unsatisfactory solution to the problem of overcriminalization. By allowing the police to decide on an ad hoc basis which laws will be enforced, it in effect makes the police the lawmakers. In addition, the broad discretion which police assume under selective enforcement policies is often exercised in a highly arbitrary manner."[22]

Partly as a result of sharp increases in the Black and Latin populations of major urban areas, the control over some of these activities has shifted in directions which have proved disturbing and unnerving to the old-line leadership. Not unnaturally, some of the residents of ghettos have demanded a larger piece of the action, no longer satisfied to remain in the lower echelons on the street. Coming out of the ghetto gangs of the 1950s, some of New York's Blacks and Puerto Ricans have risen to the higher and more profitable levels of organized crime. The *Los Angeles Times* of July 30, 1971 reported that "out of the profits from narcotics and gambling, the most successful live in the suburbs, own summer resorts, apartment houses, limousine services, strings of bars." The consultant to the New York Legislative Committee on Crime regards this as simply another to-be-expected instance of a common phenomenon: "What's happening in the illegal professions is no different than in the legal ones. Black and Spanish-speaking criminals, who have for some time been within the structure and around the periphery of organized crime, are pushing for their rights and seeking upward mobility." In the Buffalo area, numbers bets are "banked" by Blacks, with a 10 percent fee to white organized crime, and there are indications that even the 10 percent is being phased out.

Loose syndicates of neighborhood narcotics and gambling "businessmen" control operations in key sections of cities like New York, Detroit, Buffalo, Cleveland, Philadelphia, and Chicago. The membership of the Minority Mafia is estimated to number between 5000 and 10,000 and violence is on the rise as syndicates fight to protect their territories. Ironically, it is speculated that the new indigenous crime leaders may be partly responsible for keeping the ghettos cool, because riots can be bad for business. Corrupt police now solicit bribes directly from the ghetto leaders, having learned that this is a source of power and wealth. The reason cited by the correspondent for the growth of minority organized crime is consistent with the basic analysis of this study: crime is a fast route out of the ghetto and into the suburbs, and for young people the lure is especially strong.

The historical pattern of the development and function of the subeconomy is now somewhat clear. Its important characteristics can be delineated thus:

(1) The economy has usually served a recognized and pervasive consumer demand, and in many fundamental respects it performs the same functions as the "legitimate" market. Satisfaction of that demand can only be accomplished through the subeconomy because, ordinarily for moral reasons, the sale of the product or the performance of the service has been formally outlawed, or in the case of the political machine, the activity involved was believed to violate sound economic principles.

(2) The subeconomy has most conspicuously functioned in areas of the city inhabited by members of some minority group, though frequently it has served the needs of groups living elsewhere. The

locus of the subeconomy in such areas is satisfying to the dominant majority and the political structure which is responsive to the interests of that majority, because the minorities assume the major risks and also because the identification of that minority with "crime" helps support the prejudices of the majority and the resulting structure of discrimination which again serves its desires and needs.

(3) The general public easily tolerates the subeconomy whenever the accompanying violence and "immorality" are kept within the confines of the ghetto. When they break out of the ghetto and invade Anglo neighborhoods, the public has usually responded in two ways: a) it demands stronger and more repressive law enforcement in terms which will force violent crime out of its neighborhoods and back into the ghetto, and b) it seeks a liberalization of law and law enforcement in those cases where members of the *majority* group, notably the younger persons, might otherwise be branded as law violators. A particularly apt example of the latter tendency occurred in California in 1968, at a time when the use of marijuana had become increasingly widespread in Anglo middle-class communities. In that year the state legislature softened the penalty for its use by allowing judges and juries to treat first-offense possession of marijuana as a misdemeanor rather than as a mandatory felony. In my judgment, that liberalization probably would not have occurred if marijuana usage had remained essentially a ghetto phenomenon.[23]

(4) Another reason for the tolerance of the general public, given the above constraints, is that much of the income and wealth generated by illegal economic activity flows or remains outside of the ghetto. As illustrated in the previous chapter, the American drug industry has profited immeasurably from the growing market for pills, many of which are sold and obtained illegally. There have sometimes been direct ties between certain elements of the subeconomy and legitimate business. A few decades ago, for instance, the Ford Motor Company's service department employed leading racketeers, including the notorious Joe Adonis. One Detroit ringleader was a partner in a Ford agency and owned a fruit concession at Ford's River Rouge plant. The alliances in the garment industry, previously cited, offer another example.[24]

(5) The survival of the subeconomy depends upon the appropriate cooperation from the police and the local and/or national

political administrations. The police and some of the politicians traditionally share in the proceeds of the subeconomy, which are considerable. Several years ago, Elmo Roper estimated that "only the food, steel, auto, chemical, and machine-tool industries have a greater volume of business" than gambling in this country.

(6) For some, the subeconomy has been the most readily visible route to economic success. The ghetto youngster, in particular, has historically perceived this as the way to secure a high income within a reasonably short period of time. At least until recently, however, the Black and Brown minorities have participated in profits only at the lower levels. Because of the selective enforcement of law, the major dealers are only occasionally penalized, but youngsters on the street will usually pick up an arrest record for possession of marijuana. There is some evidence that the Blacks and Browns are moving up the ladder of organized crime, though as far as I can tell this applies more to Eastern cities than to Los Angeles as of the present time.

(7) The operation of the subeconomy has allowed the majority group to perpetuate and strengthen its control over employment practices and the allocation of jobs in the legitimate sector of the economy, for the reason that minority-group involvement in illegal economic activities (plus, in recent years, the payment of welfare allowances at a low income level) has produced some income for minorities without requiring the majority to make available many of the legal jobs which it has traditionally controlled. Furthermore, penalties for low level participation in the subeconomy (jail terms, arrest and conviction records, narcotics addiction, etc.) necessarily impose special burdens upon the participants whenever they seek or temporarily obtain better legitimate jobs. Hence the combination of these factors, together with the seniority advantages already accumulated by the permanently and legitimately employed Anglos, effectively forces some minorities to remain in the subeconomy as the only means of survival. A further exploration of some aspects of this problem is contained in the next chapter.

(8) Sociologist Daniel Bell has observed, correctly in my judgment, that crime has been part of the American way of life, as a channel for some of the violent (sometimes repressed) impulses in the American character and as a means of achieving social mobility for many who are unwilling or unable to use the more normal routes. Many American fortunes have been built on a

foundation of corruption, manipulation, violence, and fraud. The early settlers and the founders of the West, Bell comments, "often did so by shady speculations and a not inconsiderable amount of violence. They ignored, circumvented, or stretched the law when it stood in the way of America's destiny and their own—or were themselves the law when it served their purposes. This has not prevented them and their descendants from feeling proper moral outrage when, under the changed circumstances of the crowded urban environments, latecomers pursued equally ruthless tactics."[25]

It might be inferred, from our analysis of the history of the subeconomy, that the Blacks and the Browns can transfer out of the ghetto economy in much the same way as the previous immigrant groups escaped into the mainstream of the society. Professor Handlin, as one example, believes that the process of adjustment for Negroes and Puerto Ricans in New York has been, and will continue to be, essentially similar to that experienced by the earlier groups. Over time, then, a process of assimilation and increasing social mobility will ease the tensions that now exist and complete the necessary adjustment of the newer migrants to the city.

There are certainly obvious similarities in the problems faced by the various groups. However, the various difficulties encountered by the Negroes, Chicanos and Puerto Ricans appear to be substantially more complex than those which confronted their predecessors.[26] A few of these obstacles can be categorized in the following terms:

(1) In some cases the physical characteristics of the previous immigrant groups made it easier for them to assimilate into the Anglo mainstream. Name changes, religious conversions, and so forth often were sufficient to give the group members acceptance by and access to the majority culture. In the case of the Blacks and, in some instances, the Chicanos and Puerto Ricans, their appearance and thus their visibility as a distinct group cannot be so readily altered.[27]

(2) The previous immigrant groups came into the urban areas voluntarily, with their families intact and usually with a sense of community and cultural solidarity. To a degree, it might be argued that their role as minorities in an often hostile environment strengthened their sense of community and their incentive to overcome discrimination. Their strong family ties were particularly

important to the children and younger members of the group, as they began to seek education and social mobility.

The experience of the Blacks was precisely the reverse. Originally they came to the country as slaves; families were deliberately and cruelly broken apart and their culture undermined for reasons both malicious and well intentioned. They were forbidden to seek the kind of ethnic or cultural solidarity which the other groups brought with them to the United States. The social and economic denigration of the Black male continued after the abolition of slavery, and the effects of this experience are felt even today.

(3) The economic circumstances surrounding the introduction of earlier groups into the American economy were more favorable than they are today. Some of the immigrant groups, for example the Jews, contained many who had at least a measure of skill in a trade or a small business or profession. There was in general a pervasive demand for unskilled labor, which does not exist in that degree today. Even if all minimum wage laws were repealed, it is doubtful that the economy would spontaneously generate enough employment for all of the unskilled and poorly educated youngsters in the labor market, except possibly under conditions equal to those prevailing during World War II, which are inflationary in the extreme.

(4) Though the other groups carried the heavy burden of invidious stereotypes (aside from religious prejudices, the Irish were characterized as "drunkards," the Italians as "criminal," and the Jews as "cunning and clannish"), only the Blacks have been historically categorized by a White culture as *biologically* inferior. The alleged defects of the others could be interpreted as merely cultural in origin; there were, perhaps, some who believed that the Irish were congenitally alcoholic and the Italians congenitally criminal, but there has not been a general belief, and attempt to demonstrate, that their *intelligence* is inferior to that of Anglo-Saxons for genetic reasons. The historical compulsion of Whites to treat Negroes as if they were mentally inferior has been occasioned, in large part, by the need to justify first the enslavement of and later the massive discrimination against Black people in this country. The net result of this pattern has been that the intensity of expressed racial prejudice against the minority in question has been far greater in the case of Blacks than in any other case.

(5) In return, there has been an inevitable and completely

natural counterreaction among the Blacks, and particularly the young Blacks. Because of the majority efforts to destroy their culture (or, in some cases, the denial that Blacks have had or could have a culture) and the past or contemporaneous attempts to picture them as inferior in some sense, many Blacks now assert a fierce and profound racial or cultural pride which makes them even more resistant to the tvpical assimilationist arguments. To some degree this has brought them into conflict not only with the conservatives but with those liberals who regard themselves as "integrationists"—a label which implies to many, among Blacks and Anglos alike, that the minority will be permitted full and nondiscriminatory access to the cultural mainstream.

The consequence of these unique events and processes has been that Blacks, and to a somewhat lesser extent the Browns, face special problems in the labor market which have not similarly burdened the older migrant groups. In the next chapter, I shall discuss these problems in some detail and argue that the minority *young man* is their greatest victim.

NOTES

1. Andrew Sinclair, *Prohibition: The Era of Excess*, Boston: Little, Brown, 1962, p. 220.
2. D. P. Moynihan, "The Irish," a chapter in *Beyond the Melting Pot*, by Nathan Glazer and D. P. Moynihan. Cambridge: MIT Press and Harvard University Press, 1963, p. 224.
3. *Ibid.*, p. 255.
4. Daniel Bell, *The End of Ideology*, New York: Collier, 1962 (revised), p. 131.
5. John Landesco, "Prohibition and Crime," *Annals of the American Academy of Political and Social Science*, September 1932, p. 124, quoted in Andrew Sinclair, *Prohibition: The Era of Excess,* p. 226.
6. Andrew Sinclair, *Prohibition: The Era of Excess*, pp. 226-227.
7. Nathan Glazer and D. P. Moynihan, *Beyond the Melting Pot*, Cambridge: MIT Press and Harvard University Press, 1963, p. 184.
8. Nathan Glazer and D. P. Moynihan, *Beyond the Melting Pot* (2nd ed., 1970), p. 211.
9. Daniel Bell, *The End of Ideology*, p. 147.
10. Andrew Sinclair, *Prohibition: The Era of Excess*, pp. 229-230.
11. In 1943 a wire tap on the phone of racketeer Frank Costello revealed that a nominee to the Supreme Court of the State of New York had thanked Costello for arranging the appointment. This is but one example among many illustrating the close connections between organized crime and the political establishment. See Daniel Bell, *The End of Ideology*, p. 145.
12. Oscar Handlin, *The Newcomers*, New York: Anchor Books, 1959, pp. 102-103.
13. *Wall Street Journal*, November 22, 1971, editorial page, excerpt from

the book *Dealer: Portrait of a Cocaine Merchant*, by Richard Woodley. The previous quote from Clarence Williams III I have constructed from my memory of his conversation on a recent Dick Cavett television show.

14. "Police Crime: More Than 'Rotten Apples,'" *Wall Street Journal*, November 22, 1971, editorial page. A UPI dispatch to the *Los Angeles Times* earlier in 1971, quoted the testimony of a young New York patrolman that "of the 70 patrolmen he worked with in a Brooklyn ghetto, all but two took bribes." Another police force veteran and former FBI agent also testified that corruption was widespread, with "shakedowns and bribes running into the millions of dollars."

15. *The Police and the Public*, New Haven: Yale University Press, 1971, pp. 175-176.

16. *Ibid.*, p. 160. Reiss' discussion of officer violations of the law may be found on pp. 156-163 of his book.

17. *Crime in America.* New York: Pocket Books, 1971, pp. 79-80.

18. *Ibid.*, p. 54.

19. Richard Dougherty, "The New York Police," *Atlantic Monthly*, February 1972, p. 10. See also *Newsweek*, April 10, 1972, pp. 46-52. A UPI dispatch to the *Los Angeles Times* of July 15, 1971, notes the irony that the United States Government itself formally participates in the profits of the subeconomy through its collection of taxes on the illegal sale or purchase of marijuana.

20. *New Perspectives on Urban Crime*, American Bar Association, 1972, p. 16ff. In addition to the chairman, committee members are as follows: Circuit Judge Edward Allen Tamm, former Assistant to the FBI Director; Joseph A. Califano, Jr., Special Assistant for Domestic Affairs to President Lyndon Johnson; Samuel Dash, Professor of Criminal Law at Georgetown University and formerly District Attorney of Philadelphia; Frank S. Hogan, District Attorney for the County of New York; Charles H. Rogovin, President of the Police Foundation; John J. Sullivan, past president of the Chicago Bar Association; Fred M. Vinson, Jr., formerly Assistant Attorney General; James Vorenberg, Professor of Criminal Law at Harvard University and Executive Director of the 1967 President's Commission on Law Enforcement and Administration of Justice.

21. *Ibid.*, p. 21. The previous long quotation may be found on p. 20 of the report.

22. *Ibid.*, p. 22. As an illustration of the waste in judicial resources associated with overcriminalization, the ABA committee notes that in 1969 almost one quarter of all arrests in the United States were for drunkenness. In 1970 more than one third of all felony arrests in Los Angeles were related to the possession of marijuana.

23. Indeed, actions by the California legislature illustrate *both* aspects of majority reaction to drug usage. The legislature had toughened the penalty for marijuana possession, in line with the usual first response described above. When this failed to restrict usage to the "traditional" areas, the second type of response was made. Note the incisive comment on this point, made by a ghetto teenager in the previous chapter.

24. Andrew Sinclair, *Prohibition: The Era of Excess*, pp. 224-225, on the Ford Service Department. The quotation from Elmo Roper is from Daniel Bell, *The End of Ideology*, p. 133.

25. Daniel Bell, *The End of Ideology*, p. 148.

26. It should also be noted that, even in the case of the Irish and Italian Catholics and the Jews, noticeable vestiges of prejudice and discrimination

against them persist to this day, though in strictly economic terms they have progressed markedly.

27. This should not be interpreted to mean that I approve of this form of "forced assimilation" on the majority's terms. To the contrary, I regard it not only as malicious and discriminatory but as socially counterproductive. However, much of the "assimilationist" argument implies that it is necessary, if not desirable.

# 9

## SPECIAL OBSTACLES TO YOUTH EMPLOYMENT

There are certain labor market obstacles confronting *any* young man, regardless of his race or national origin or general economic status. His age alone puts him at a disadvantage with many employers, who would prefer someone with greater maturity and experience. Unless he has special training or education, he is likely to be relegated to specified unskilled jobs which provide low pay and little advancement opportunity. To many young men, however, this process has its advantages and benefits, aside from the immediate income it offers. The work serves as an introduction to the labor market and to job routine, and even if his own employment is at a low level, the youngster often has a chance to observe other jobs—clerical, semiskilled, skilled, and even managerial and professional—which might interest and intrigue him in the longer run.

Usually the income from his employment is not crucial to the livelihood of his household, because his father is fully employed with earnings sufficient to meet the basic needs of the family. The youngster's wages are supplementary, designed to satisfy some extra needs of his own. To be sure, there are cases in which his earnings are essential to the continuation and completion of his education, and there are low-income households in which the family's welfare depends on his contributions. In one way or another, most of the households in Watts and east Los Angeles fall in this last category.

A conventional view of unemployment in the central city ghetto is that the problem, particularly as it affects young people, is a common and persistent historical phenomenon, much aggravated now by the impacts of minimum wage legislation, technological innovation leading to job displacement, and cultural factors arising from the resistance of many Blacks and Browns to assimilation into the mainstream culture. Some have argued that other ethnic minorities have also faced discrimination and poverty and that the young men of Watts and east Los Angeles could follow the successful path blazed by their ethnic predecessors. With appropriate overhaul of minimum-wage policy and other interferences with

**Table 11.**

*Perceived Obstacles to Career, by Area*

|  | East Los Angeles | South Los Angeles |
|---|---|---|
| *Arrests and convictions* | | |
| Total number of respondents | 33 | 9 |
| Misdemeanor only | 18 | 1 |
| Felony only | 10 | 5 |
| Combination of misdemeanor & felony | 4 | 0 |
| Unable to determine degree of crime | 1 | 3 |
| *Not enough schooling or lack of education* | | |
| Total number of respondents | 9 | 57 |
| *Difficulty in reading* | | |
| Total number of respondents | 0 | 4 |
| *Location of jobs in relation to residence* | | |
| Total number of respondents | 3 | 0 |
| *Discrimination* | | |
| Total number of respondents | 6 | 2 |
| *Other* | | |
| Total number of respondents | 2 | 4 |
| *Any combination of reasons stated above* | | |
| Total number of respondents | 4 | 20* |

\* For SLA, combinations stated were as follows:

| Discrimination & school | 10 |
|---|---|
| Discrimination & arrest | 7 |
| Discrimination, school, & reading | 2 |
| Discrimination & reading | 1 |

free competition, the youngsters presumably could get jobs and enter careers by pursuing educational goals and adjusting to the norms of the established market.

This assumes that the labor-market problems of Black and Brown young men are essentially the same as those confronting the members of immigrant groups who themselves have been herded into big-city ghettos and discriminated against, with the important qualification that large-scale economic and technological changes have now eliminated many of the unskilled jobs that were formerly available. Nevertheless, the burdens carried by the youngsters we have surveyed are not *simply* those carried by their ethnic predecessors but are special and unique in several respects.

Combining the results of our survey in both Watts and east Los Angeles, we find that lack of education was rated as the foremost obstacle to achievement of career goals, followed by arrests and convictions, discrimination, difficulty in reading, and job location, in that order.

## Arrest and Conviction Records

The police record is a burden which many young men in Watts and east Los Angeles must carry, and its impact on employability is overwhelming. Whatever the rationalizations offered by police officials for the fact, it is clear and undeniable that the Black or Brown young man in a low-income ghetto or barrio is far more likely to be detained and arrested than is an Anglo youngster anywhere else in the city. He may or may not have been guilty of a crime, and the detention may or may not result in a formal arrest. If it does, the arrest may remain a stain on his record throughout his life, even though the charge is dropped or he is subsequently acquitted.[1]

This becomes more burdensome in the current labor market if the charge involves narcotics, as it does in an extremely high percentage of all alleged offenses in the ghetto or barrio. Ironically the so-called victimless crimes are sometimes a greater deterrent to employment than are the crimes against persons or property. Offenses such as possession of marijuana, possession of dangerous drugs, indecent exposure, and so forth may automatically be regarded by employers as indications of moral or emotional unreliability, despite the fact that such a premise has never been validated.

Many employers, private and public, continue to require preemployment information on both arrests and convictions, even including those arrests which were dismissed without trial. Some governmental jurisdictions and private business firms have now eliminated from their employment application forms those questions relating entirely to arrests not followed by convictions, thus conforming to a policy recommended by the Equal Employment Opportunity Commission, the California Fair Employment Practice Commission, and other antidiscrimination agencies. Nevertheless, a great many employers continue to require this information, and even among those who formally do not, it would appear that some proportion of them acquire these facts clandestinely through their background record checks of job applicants. Most criminal record sheets, available from various law enforcement agencies, list *all* arrests and convictions, and an employer who so inquired could learn of mere arrests through this channel even though he never directly questions the applicant. Only those records of criminal charges which have been sealed by court order would be unavailable to the inquiring employer.

In its official preemployment inquiries guide, the California FEPC has suggested the following wording: "Have you ever been convicted of any crime? If so, when, where, and disposition of case?" The wording actually used by certain large employers varies considerably, as the sampling below will show:

*Certified Grocers of California*: Have you ever been arrested, indicted, or convicted of any crime?

*North American Rockwell*: Have you ever been arrested, charged or held, even though dismissed, by any law enforcement authority, for any violation of law? Include all courtsmartial while in military service. Do not include traffic violations for which the only penalty imposed was a fine of $50 or less. If Yes, give date, place, charge and disposition under "Remarks".

*Nissan Motor Corporation* [*Datsun*]: Have you ever been convicted by Federal, State, or other Law Enforcement Authorities for any violation of Federal, State, County or Municipal Law, Regulation, Ordinance, or any Law? Include all courts-martial while in Military Service. Do not include anything that happened before your 16th birthday. Do not include traffic violations for which the only penalty imposed was a fine of $25.00 or less. If Yes, give date, place, charge and disposition.

*Bank of America*: Have you ever been arrested for other than a minor traffic offense?

*American District Telegraph Company*: Have you ever been convicted of a criminal offense? If so, attach statement of particulars.

*McDonnell-Douglas*: Have you ever been arrested, convicted, charged or held by federal, state, or other law enforcement authorities, for any violation of any federal law, state law, county or municipal law, regulation, or ordinance or any other law? Include all court martials while in United States military service. Do not include anything that happened before your 16th birthday. Do not include traffic violations for which the only penalty imposed was a fine of $25 or less. All other charges must be included even if they were dismissed. If Yes, give date, place, charge, and disposition.

A massive study of hiring policies of state, county and local governments, focused on the question of how arrest and conviction records might relate to public employment, has recently been commissioned by the U. S. Department of Labor. Supervised by Herbert S. Miller of the Institute of Criminal Law and Procedure of the Georgetown University Law Center in Washington, D. C., the study concludes that most jurisdictions require preemployment information on both arrests and convictions and that the resulting discrimination against applicants with records probably has an important employment impact.[2]

In the words of the report: "Almost one fifth of the jurisdictions and agencies reported that an arrest record was an absolute bar to employment. Virtually all reported that they do consider some kind of criminal record as possible grounds for not hiring. Most agencies and jurisdictions (except the police) did not indicate the specific type of criminal record considered. But it is a fair inference that they were not limiting themselves to records of convictions, especially when considered in the light of on-site interviews and the finding that most jurisdictions ask about arrest records. Most police agencies explicitly indicated that they do not limit themselves to conviction records. Half the responding police agencies consider records of legal involvement short of conviction."[3]

Since that report on the problem is now available generally, my own comments here will be limited to its possible implication for the young residents of Watts and east Los Angeles. In theory certain of the offenses committed under the age of 21 can be officially sealed, and except for such records as are kept by federal departments (such as the FBI) or other nonstate and nonlocal agencies, this sealing process effectively denies access to any information relative to the particular crimes. In practice, very few of the young men are even cognizant of this possibility, and as far as I can determine, only a comparative handful in Watts and east Los Angeles ever benefit from it concretely.

Even through California's expungement and sealing provisions are regarded as more liberal than those in any other state, their effectiveness is quite limited. The exoffender himself must initiate the action through a petition to the court, after a prescribed period of time has elapsed since the completion of his sentence. During this period, of course, he must not have accumulated additional offenses on his record. In principle the probation officer should fully inform the youngster of his rights under this law and voluntarily assist him in preparing the petition to the court at the appropriate time, but in my observation this is rarely done. Many persons are under the impression that they require the services of a lawyer in order to have their records sealed or expunged, and needless to say, that cost is considered prohibitive. In most cases the ex-offender knows nothing about the provision, or does not understand it if someone has mentioned it.[4]

The scope of the law is restricted, at best. For those who were between the ages of 18 and 20 at the time of the offense and whose cases were handled in adult court, only misdemeanor offenses may be sealed. Under no circumstances does the present law permit the sealing or expungement of narcotics, traffic, and certain sex offenses. Thus, even if full advantage were taken of the provision as it now stands, the marijuana offenses for which many youngsters are arrested would not be covered.

Another irony is that no adult can ever succeed in erasing his arrest record even though he is entirely the victim of mistaken identity. The provisions are broader and more liberal with respect to those cases handled in juvenile court, but as noted, many youngsters are simply unaware of their existence or remain ineligible because of repeated offenses. Legislation to liberalize the provisions of the penal code has been introduced in recent sessions of the California legislature, but it has aroused consistent opposition from some law enforcement officials and has never been enacted.[5]

In California there also are provisions which allow adult offenders to petition for the withdrawal of their guilty pleas or the setting aside of guilty verdicts, but only after they have completed probation (except that misdemeanor offenders not granted probation may obtain expungement upon a showing of good conduct for at least a year after termination of sentence). This peculiar law, as far as I can ascertain, does not seal the record in question, but only restores to the successful petitioner certain of his civil rights. The record itself remains open to all those who are entitled to see it (presumably with a notation of the court action). Furthermore, it has been pointed out that all such "laws apparently allow an employer or licensing agency to compel a former offender to disclose whether he has ever *sought* the relief provided by the statute" (emphasis added).[6]

There are wide gaps between official policy and practice in the area of criminal records. Although the Los Angeles Police Commission many years ago adopted a policy that the records kept by the Los Angeles police department are to be revealed only to the appropriate law enforcement or judicial officers, employers have informed me several times that their security divisions are regularly able to secure access to those records for purposes of employment checking. Naturally there are sources available to them even if the police department enforced the policy in its own department. Officials of other police departments or law enforcement offices can readily secure the necessary information and pass it along to friendly employers, or the company personnel department possibly can get it from the files of the FBI or the state attorney general's office. Many companies recruit ex-policemen or ex-FBI agents as their head security officers, partly because they are in an unusually good position to obtain this and similar information.

A recent court decision in the District of Columbia (*Menard vs. Mitchell,* June 15, 1971) has ruled that the FBI files are not open to governmental units which seek them only for purposes of checking applications for employment or licenses. This decision, if not overturned, could have enormous implications for exoffenders who apply for jobs in agencies where personnel departments have normally checked FBI records. In addition a 1970 decision of the United States District Court in Los Angeles, in the case of *Gregory vs. Litton Systems, Inc.*, applies the Civil Rights Act of 1964 to employers who require job applicants to list arrests not followed by convictions, on the grounds that Blacks are arrested more often than are Whites and that, in the absence of a showing that the hiring policy is actually a business necessity, the requirement constitutes *de facto* discrimination against Negroes within the meaning of the act. In this case the applicant had been denied employment solely on the basis of the number of his arrests, and had initiated a civil suit for damages. Litton Systems, however, has appealed this verdict.[7]

Professor Miller and his associates at Georgetown attribute much significance to the Litton decision and regard it as a highly useful precedent for public policy. They believe that it has potentially wide application, but recommend specific federal legislation prohibiting the use of arrest records for employment purposes. The Georgetown Institute also proposes model statutes for the sealing and expungement of criminal records at the state level, where, of course, the greatest impact occurs. The American Bar Association has been granted a contract by the Manpower Administration to establish an information clearinghouse on job restrictions for exoffenders.[8]

Senator Quentin Burdick of North Dakota has introduced legislation (S. 2732, known as the Offender Rehabilitation Act) to expunge the records of rehabilitated offenders who have committed no more than one offense. This legislation, of course, would apply only to the convicted violators of federal laws, but Senator Burdick is hopeful that it will serve as a useful precedent as well as meeting some substantive needs in the federal courts. Among the reasons for enactment of the law, he cites the favorable experience of the Department of Labor in securing bonding for former offenders who complete training programs.

During the four-year period over which I have had occasion to explore some aspects of this problem, I have consistently been told by representatives of licensing agencies and of personnel departments, public and private, that they consider each application on its merits, and except where required by law or administrative practice, employment is not automatically denied to the ex-offender. The statements of ex-offenders, and my own observations, dispute this contention. One young man from east Los Angeles told me that he had recently tested the policy of the Los Angeles Board of Education; he had submitted his application for a playground job, having been advised to apply and to include a full account of his record, and then was turned down because he had a record.

In an attempt to discover what guidelines, if any, are applied by public agencies in determining which applicants with records are acceptable and which ones are not, I have made inquiry on several occasions and have never ascertained what those guidelines may be or whether they exist at all. The implication is that the personnel officer makes a separate and subjective decision in each individual case, based on his judgment and experience. This would appear to be both administratively infeasible and highly arbitrary. It seems likely that the applicant with a felony record will be hired only when there are special circumstances in his favor, and that he always remains at a critical disadvantage in comparison with those applicants whose records are clean. Jurisdictions such as the county government of Los Angeles have even required job applicants to list those adult offenses which have been "expunged" under the provision allowing petitions for the setting aside of guilty verdicts.

A few personal examples can illustrate, better than any abstractions, the impact of contemporary police and legal practices upon ghetto or barrio youngsters. Let us take the case (a real one) of a young man who is picked up by the Los Angeles police as a robbery suspect. The suspicion is false, but before he is released, his car has been impounded and he has had to pay a hefty impound charge, out of a not very large income, to regain possession of it; he has been temporarily jailed and has lost time from work; and he has accumulated another arrest on his record which is totally unjustified but can never be erased.

Here is another example drawn from the author's direct knowledge. A policeman has arrested a gentle and conscientious young man of Watts, on the probably baseless charge of plain drunkenness, after verbally harassing the youngster and his younger brother. He is taken to jail at the 77th Street precinct station near Watts, and his mother, who is on welfare, must bail him out in the middle of the night. He receives a notice to appear at a hearing, in a judicial facility located about fifteen miles from Watts, and he is without transportation. He misses the hearing because a clerical error by the police has recorded the wrong hearing date on his notice, and his absence means that he is automatically adjudged guilty and the bail is forfeited. This is a misdemeanor, and there is no further legal action against him, but, of course, he now has a drunkenness conviction on his record and has never had a chance to plead innocent to the charge because of a police error. The error is discovered, by accident, after the correct hearing date has already passed. As the young man's friend, I explore the situation and after several phone calls and much wasted time, finally reach someone who verifies the error. The mistake is clearly a responsibility of the police and the courts, and has effectively deprived him of his legal rights.

What can be done? The bureaucrat in the distant office tries to be helpful, but he is nonplussed. He says that he really is not sure what might be done about it, but probably the young man could come to the office, verify the mistake in person, and fill out a form attesting to it. This would be a fifteen-mile trip for him (and he has no car), in order *perhaps* to rectify an error originally made by the police. It is doubtful that he can ever erase the stain from his record; at best the effort would consume endless hours and entail an unnerving battle with the bureaucracy. The process ends with the phone call. He never made the trip, and a mistake-prone typist has succeeded in wiping out his constitutional rights.

The chances of being arrested at least once are many times greater for a Black or Chicano youngster in Watts and east Los Angeles than they are for their Anglo counterparts. Because of this inescapable fact, the Black and Chicano must often pay out money for bail bonds or fines, or stay in jail (possibly endangering his job) even though he is eventually adjudged innocent. With the usual traffic offenses, the fines will sometimes go unpaid and warrants will be issued for the arrest of the offenders. Thus the same vicious circle recurs again and again, and the young man finds that the legal system is stacked against him.

## Discrimination

Discrimination still is perceived as an obstacle by many, more so by Blacks than by Chicanos, but the perception is most directly related to educational and police practices and to housing segregation. The reason for this is apparent: the actual labor-market experience of many youngsters is limited, and they will rarely encounter *overt* signs of racial discrimination in hiring. On the other hand, they have had ample opportunity to observe and evaluate the impact of education and law enforcement, and the evidence of residential segregation is everywhere.

Each facet of discrimination is translated into a labor-market equivalent. Inequitable police policies give rise to criminal records, or mere arrest records, which in turn are used by employers to deny employment to the applicant (as noted in the previous section). Inadequate or ineffective education will bar the youngster from those jobs carrying rigid educational stipulations, or cause him to fail the standard preemployment tests, or impair the quality of his job performance if he should reach that level. Housing segregation denies him a realistic chance to move closer to many of the centers of potential employment, and transportation is both costly and inefficient.

The question raised earlier is whether this pattern is different in any fundamental way from that experienced by earlier immigrant groups in the United States, understanding as we must that the Blacks and Browns can also be regarded as "immigrant" groups because they are migrants to large urban communities from the rural South or from Mexico. Professor Banfield and his cohorts have argued that American society has advanced to a point where racial discrimination is no longer a major problem and that minority youngsters must themselves be held responsible for whatever maladjustments they suffer in the labor market. Several of our interviewees would agree that the road ahead is clear and that they can travel as far as their own initiative and ability can carry them. My own estimation of their prospects is that as of now their future success or failure in economic terms is strongly correlated with their capacity to assimilate into the so-called cultural mainstream, and that this process remains a great deal more difficult for Blacks and for many Browns than it has been for minorities such as the Irish, Italians, and Jews. Further, I suspect that the Blacks in particular have been allowed less independence and flexibility than have the ethnic immigrants; in a sense, the Negro has had to become "more white than the whites" as a minimum condition for economic and political acceptance.

This is generally confirmed by an examination of the history of minorities in New York City. There is little evidence that a bitter antagonism prevailed between the police and minority communities as it does now in Watts and east Los Angeles, at least in the case of young men. The Irish, indeed, moved in large numbers into the police department, and this became one of their earliest routes to economic security. While many of the East Side neighborhoods were characterized by petty crime and street hustling, the Jews were not excessively burdened by criminal records. Oscar Handlin argues that the Jews moved up the economic ladder faster than did the Irish or the Italians, who were encumbered with strictly cultural impediments to interest in and entry into the professions and business. The Italian youngsters, to be sure, did sometimes come into conflict with the law, but often it was in the context of an economy and a community which tolerated their crime. Under any circumstances, historians seem to agree that their slower ascent in the labor market was due to cultural and educational factors and not primarily to difficulties with the law.

Questions of education and housing patterns must be viewed as a package, because the importance of the neighborhood school in American life means that one's ability to secure the highest available quality of education for himself or for his children is related in large part to his mobility. In the past, Jews have encountered discriminatory barriers at the college level, particularly at certain of the professional schools and departments, but according to Professor Handlin, their adjustment to the public school was relatively quick and successful, and their occupational and residential mobility was reasonably unimpaired within the metropolitan New York area.[9] In the cases of all minorities, however, neighborhood concentrations have persisted to this day, and a cultural pluralism has fundamentally modified and diluted the "melting" or assimilation process. Thus, at best, these minorities have been permitted some freedom of choice with respect to their retention or abandonment of cultural ties, and the degree of their ethnic uniqueness. The intensity of Anglo hostility to movements for community control and cultural nationalism in Black and Brown areas—often categorized as "separatist" in motivation—suggests to me that the same degree of independence has not been accorded to those whom Professor Handlin terms the newest immigrants.[9]

The most reasonable inference from this historical review, in my judgment, is that the young men in Watts and east Los Angeles suffer all of the problems endured by the immigrant minorities, but in the case of the Blacks, each problem has been exacerbated and supplemented by others endemic to their own experience. The issue as it affects Chicanos is less clear to me; the intensity of discrimination against them in the labor market does not appear to be quite as great, and their residential patterns in Los Angeles reflect more dispersion and mobility than is true in the case of the Blacks. Nevertheless, the problems in east Los Angeles are about as acute and complex as they are in Watts, notably in the educational and law enforcement fields. Also, in some respects the Spanish-speaking groups are often regarded as more alien than are the Blacks. The fact that the Spanish-speaking peoples long preceded the Anglos as residents of the Southwest does not seem to be given much weight.

This should not be viewed as a counsel of despair. To the contrary, I am sanguine about the possibility of meaningful progress, *if* the Anglos are prepared to accept and implement the conditions for it. The pervasiveness of concentration upon these problems has too often obscured the real strengths in the Black and Brown communities of Los Angeles, few of which have been nurtured and developed by the largely unimaginative programs initiated so far. These communities are reservoirs of great talent and human resources of enormous potential. It is merely time that they were treated as such.

NOTES

1. A great many of these detentions and arrests have been, and remain today, entirely unlawful. In a 1971 decision in the Gallik case, the California Supreme Court reaffirmed an earlier decision (*Kiefer*, December 1970) that a traffic violation is *not* a valid ground for a search of the violator's car, even if the "suspect" engages in so-called furtive gestures. This, in fact, has been and is a common police practice in Watts and east Los Angeles; indeed, many of the arrests for possession of marijuana occur precisely in this manner. However, most arrestees are advised by public defenders to plead guilty, and the defender will rarely challenge search and seizure methods effectively or appeal a guilty verdict for his "client."

2. The report is titled *The Closed Door: The Effect of a Criminal Record on Employment with State and Local Public Agencies.* Washington, D. C., Georgetown Univ. Law Center, 1972.

3. *Ibid.*, p. 100.

4. I am unsure as to whether the existing legal service offices, funded by the federal government, can legally assist the exoffender in obtaining sealing or expungement of his record. Their jurisdiction is limited to *civil* cases only, and the petitioning required is connected with a criminal offense. I can attest that no one of my acquaintance in Watts or East Los Angeles has ever requested or received assistance from that source.

5. The broadest measure—Assembly Bill 267, 1972 session—would allow the sealing of records in cases not culminating in conviction for both mis-demeanors and felonies and for both adults and minors, and would elimi-nate the existing exceptions for narcotics, sex, and traffic offenses, through amendment of the penal code.

6. Adam Gough, *The Expungement of Adjudication Records of Juvenile and Adult Offenders: A Problem of Status.* Inserted in the *Congressional Record* by Senator Quentin Burdick, October 20, 1971.

7. The final report of the Task Force on New Careers and Job Develop-ment, appointed by the Los Angeles County Commission on Crime and Delinquency, was introduced as evidence in that hearing. The report recom-mends that all employers eliminate questions relating to arrests not followed by convictions, and ask questions concerning convictions only where it has been demonstrated that the crimes are related to job performance. The author was chairman of that task force and testified in the Litton hearing.

8. Patricia Marshall, "Criminal Records and Public Jobs," *Manpower,* December 1971, p. 7. See Herbert Miller, *The Closed Door,* pp. 74-77, for the text of a model annulment and sealing statute, and pp. 155-162 for a discussion of the possible significance of the *Litton* case and needed federal action to prevent employers from requiring information on arrests not fol-lowed by convictions.

9. For an historical analysis of these patterns and experiences in New York, see Oscar Handlin's *The Newcomers,* New York: Anchor Books, 1959, pp. 24-42. In a new book, *The Great School Legend,* Colin Greer argues that, contrary to general belief, the American public schools never served *any* of the immigrant groups effectively.

# 10

## TOWARD THE FUTURE

It is surely no exaggeration to suggest that the unemployment or misemployment of young men in the central-city ghettos constitutes a critical national problem with potential for social disaster unless it is solved. The results of our work will surprise no one who has had first-hand knowledge of economic conditions in areas such as Watts and east Los Angeles, and perhaps only the magnitude of our figures on unemployment will shock anyone who is aware of the grim statistics already available from Manpower Reports and other official sources. Statisticians, of course, can always argue about questions such as the precise measurement of "unemployment" or "labor force participation" or the representativeness of any given sampling of young men, but such debate is no longer very important or relevant. What we now know about the size and nature of the problem is sufficient to justify the conclusion that it is of massive dimensions and that drastic action is required.

The traditional approach, favored by economists and policymakers alike, has emphasized "investments in human capital" through education and training. Major governmental policy over the decade of the 1960s rested on a premise that labor supply is more malleable than labor demand, and that the quality of manpower ("human capital") can be changed so as to match more effectively the needs and requirements of employers. The nature of the labor market is viewed as a constant. Thus the only variable subject to social intervention is the laborer or job-seeker himself. He must somehow be reeducated or retrained or remolded or otherwise renovated to fit whatever requirement the competitive market imposes. To put it bluntly, the orthodox economist believes that it is desirable and appropriate to change human beings to meet the needs of the labor market, but rarely or never permissible to change the market to meet the needs of human beings. The demand for labor, presumably, results from an interplay of competitive forces and productivity—a process not to be disturbed or upset by government.

Those few recent attempts to intervene in the area of labor demand tend to be marginal in scope and impact. The greatest emphasis, by far, has been given to legislative and administrative programs designed to eradicate racial discrimination and thereby expand opportunities for *qualified* job applicants from minority groups. This is a highly valuable and useful effort, and indeed should be strengthened, but it seems to have only a peripheral relationship to the problems confronted by Watts and east Los Angeles youngsters. Much of the *de facto* discrimination from which they suffer is beyond the reach of Fair Employment Practice legislation. Furthermore, it is worthy of note that the sanctity of the market remains unchallenged: employers continue to establish their own qualifications for work, and the applicant must be qualified in order to be acceptable. As we have noted, many of those established qualifications reflect and implement the subtle processes of discrimination which young men endure in these communities.

More innovative efforts to generate effective demand for the services of minority young men have been limited indeed. "New Careers," "Public Service Careers," and other public service employment programs have had insufficient funding and apparently only a minimal impact upon the usual hiring and promotional policies of state and local governments, which provide the greatest amount of potential employment for the target groups. This approach naturally runs counter to the preferences and predilections of most economists because it implies deliberate job creation by government, a process which can interfere with the workings of a competitive market.

Many economists would prefer to emphasize the income maintenance approach, partly because it avoids any significant interference with the market. The orthodox economist regards the cash grant as much superior to minimum wages as a means of providing assistance to the poor; to the extent that there is a work requirement attached to the relief, the recipients would work at those jobs and under those conditions established in the labor market. If they are unemployable, they can be subsidized (at a low level of payment) while the market economy functions unimpaired and the remainder of society goes about its normal business.

It will be observed that the interests, aptitudes, and ambitions of the individual are largely irrelevant to this process. If he has an interest in and aptitude for art or music or writing, and the market currently demands aircraft assemblers, he is expected to educate and train himself for aircraft assembly. Unless that ideal circumstance arises in which there is a match between aspiration and market demand, the young man is required to obey the mandates of the market.

In practice this is a complex process because *future* demand is more relevant and meaningful than *current* demand—a fact which introduces the need for projections. The science of economic forecasting is considerably less than perfect, and the demand for labor in southern California is subject not only to the vagaries of the competitive market, but also to those of foreign policy, defense spending, environmental control, space research and development, and so forth. Such uncertainties have already caused difficulty for administrators and graduates of training programs, which have been rather heavily concentrated in those semiskilled fields strongly affected by trends in large industries such as aerospace. Our survey confirms what others have found: that unemployment has risen in these occupational categories.

Aside from the inevitable imponderables introduced by the imperfections of labor market predictions, there are important reasons for a reduction in emphasis upon training programs in the mechanical trades and similar efforts on the labor supply side. Whatever value they may have in certain ways, the "investments in human capital" have not solved, or even seriously dented, the youth unemployment problem in midcity ghettos and barrios. Programs which run counter to the major interests of the target group are always vulnerable and inadequate in vital respects. Both the Parnes study and our own show that the aspirations of young men, black and white alike, predominantly do not lie in the mechanical trades. Instead, they prefer fields such as professional and technical, government, business, esthetics and entertainment, and the *higher* levels of service occupations (correctional work, etc.). There will be tangible value in shifting to programs and policies which are consistent with, rather than antagonistic to, the major interests and career goals of young men.

Certainly, as Professor Parnes has commented, at least some of those aspiring to professional and technical work are doomed to disappointment, because the most optimistic projections do not suggest a sufficiency of employment in that field to satisfy the hopes of all those aspiring to enter it. Nevertheless, the professional, technical and service occupations will grow faster than any other group: the professional and technical category alone will expand by 50 percent by 1980, and the service occupations will grow by 45 percent. State and local governments will be important sources of employment, with a projected 52 percent increase in the 1970s. It would seem feasible and desirable to augment those programs directed to the goal of employing much higher proportions of minority youngsters in the white-collar fields, notably in the governmental sector. This may well require substantial review of job standards and hiring policies in public employment, with the conscious generation of human service jobs designed with the interests and needs of minority young men in mind. Such employment would be generally consonant with increasingly vocal public demands for environmental control, improved health services, more meaningful education, safer streets, a better correctional system, and elimination of drug abuse. It would have the beneficial consequence of expanding the effective demand for young men in a variety of fields, rather than merely in those traditional vocational education areas which have received far too much emphasis already.

For those whose present aspirations cannot be satisfied in the professional and/or human service fields, obviously there must be an alternative. One clear conclusion from our survey is that all of these youngsters need and should receive more effective counseling and more comprehensive labor market information than they now do. Undoubtedly they are now inclined to specify the professional and other white-collar fields because these are prestigious and carry with them the prospects of high income, but much of this tendency probably flows from a lack of awareness of alternatives which might be more attainable and equally satisfying. However, the very youngsters who need this information the most are the ones least likely to obtain it.

Neither the schools nor the public agencies fill the voids in the labor market informational system. The minority youngster from a low-income community enters the market with minimal guidance from his home and very little from his school. The process is circular: adults who have been denied access to information and opportunities cannot then assist their children, who experience the same pattern as they begin their "careers." In many cases their earliest labor market exposure will be in the subeconomy, and the available and visible income to be derived therefrom will distort their perceptions of work and careers. Government and the larger society are active agents in this process, tolerating and even encouraging the activities of the subeconomy (drug traffic, gambling, etc.) as long as the major risks are carried by the minorities and a substantial portion of the profit flows back into "respectable" Anglo coffers. The taxpayers are thereby relieved from any responsibility for income redistribution or fundamental reforms in the structure of regular employment.

What this analysis implies is that public attention must be paid to both the labor supply and labor *demand* sides of the market, with a vastly increased emphasis on demand. Improvements in the information process are desperately needed and will be of value, but these alone are insufficient. It is probable that better and more accessible information will only aggravate frustration unless training and employment opportunities are opened up in a diversity of fields corresponding both to the interests of job-seekers and potential trends in the market. To the extent that this may demand departures from conventional labor market procedures, society should be willing to innovate.

With this in mind, we might consider a number of specific proposals for improvement in the system of labor market information and job development, particularly as it might affect the aspirations and interests of young men in Watts and east Los Angeles.

## Education and Counseling

Neither counseling nor aptitude testing is adequate in the public schools, especially when one realizes that these sources of guidance and information often must substitute for the alternative sources (such as parental advice and assistance) which exist to a far greater degree in other communities. Teacher and student awareness of career possibilities should begin in *junior* high school, and the demonstrated aptitudes and interests of the youngster should be integrated with his regular academic counseling throughout his entire school experience.

The existing instruments for testing and evaluation of aptitudes are insufficient. Tests should be constructed to measure both verbal and nonverbal skills, in a variety of fields which coincide with ranges of occupational possibilities. These should be designed to identify the cognitive styles of students, following the model of a successful program at Oakland (Michigan) Community College. The purpose of such innovation is not to pressure the student into making a definite career choice at an early age, which is unrealistic and probably quite undesirable, but simply to make him and his teachers aware of his already existing aptitudes or traits and the breadth of career opportunities to which they might relate.[1]

The schools should avoid any invidiousness, whether real or merely apparent, in the classification of students in terms of curriculum and goals. There is evidence that too sharp a distinction between college preparatory and vocational pupils, as one example, leads to perceptions of favoritism and feelings of frustration among many students who are convinced that education, at best, is directed to others and not to them. The volume and quality of counseling should be improved in ways designed to introduce maximum flexibility. So-called vocational courses should be more than just dumping grounds for youngsters categorized as poor readers; and the government can contribute to improvement in this area by subsidizing experimental programs in vocational training in high school and by helping create trade/technical colleges which are educationally worthy.[2]

While it is probably useful in the absence of any alternatives, tenth grade guidance generally accomplishes little in the way of effective career counseling. Its placement in the tenth grade means that students are marginally interested in the subject matter which seems so remote from their immediate concerns. Testing should continue to be offered in the first year of high school, but on a broad and innovative basis and with the purpose of assisting in the subsequent academic counseling of students. Instructors in senior high school should have knowledge of comparable test results in junior high school, and counselors should constantly be aware of the *general* aptitudes and career interests of those students whom they counsel.

Programs to combine education and work experience should be vastly expanded. We have previously noted the dilemma created by the fact that an expanding economy and labor market tends to draw low-income students out of school and into the market, possibly to the detriment of their longer run interests and goals. Work/study opportunities at all educational levels—from high school through graduate school—would increase the motivation of youngsters to stay in school, and at the same time could provide a valuable introduction to work and the labor market.

## Entering the Labor Market

Agencies such as the Employment Service should greatly expand and improve their community outreach services. Broad use should be made of the media, such as television and radio: regular announcements of job openings and qualifications, training programs, "New Careers" slots, and so forth should be offered in the mass media as well as in the community newspapers. In predominantly Chicano areas, of course, counselors and job development specialists should have fluency in Spanish and English. Employment Service personnel should work actively and continuously with representatives and members of community organizations— Teen Posts, boys' clubs, local centers, and even youth gangs. In a sense, the practical test of the effectiveness of a counselor or job developer in an Employment Service office should be the amount of time he spends in direct contact with youngsters on the streets or (on the other side of the coin) with employers who might be sources of employment. There should be, of course, immediate liaison between job developers and the appropriate antidiscrimination agencies, in those cases where any evidence or suspicion of racial discrimination exists.[3]

Obviously the improvement of labor market information can lead only to a dead end unless there are job or training openings to report. As we have noted before, those openings increasingly will occur in the professional, technical, and service fields, and most notably in the governmental sector of the economy. This fact suggests the need for a reorientation of training toward the paraprofessional and human service occupations, without necessarily abandoning those programs which have had success in the semiskilled or skilled fields. A compromise is necessary between the present aspirations of minority young men and the corresponding requirements of the private competitive labor market, with some redirection of career goals through counseling and some deliberate job creation in those areas where a coincidence prevails between aspirations and social need.

To the degree that society can utilize the aptitudes and meet the personal goals of Black and Brown youngsters, a felicitous accommodation of interests is possible. The young men, deprived as they have been of material possessions, are potentially eager customers for the products of the goods-producing industries, where the (mainly Anglo) semiskilled and skilled workers are now concentrated. In turn the youngsters can offer unparalleled talent in a number of fields: drama, art, music, literature, and the creative occupations generally. By using their existing skills and strengths and thereby acquiring a regular income, they can help sustain those industries which produce cars, stereo sets, houses, boats, musical instruments, and so on. As a whole, the minority young men are probably more "consumption oriented" than the Anglo kids, many of whom are rebelling against the system and materialistic values.

There are other *quid pro quos* which might be introduced into this socioeconomic calculus. In those sectors which are highly unionized, government could use a combination of carrot (subsidies) and stick (antidiscrimination policies) to induce union and employer alike to expand employment of minority youth, in the context of a general expansion of demand for the services of that industry. A useful precedent for this approach already exists in the trucking industry, where the Transportation Opportunity Program and concomitant agreements can generate jobs for Blacks and Chicanos in that same context.

Subsidies and noncompetitive job creation horrify the conventional economists, but they have been an integral and consistent part of American economic development since the founding of the Republic. Millions of Americans, over the range of economic enterprises, benefit directly or indirectly from subsidies, tax privileges, favorable government contracts, and price supports. Consumer sovereignty can be exercised through the political as well as the market process. Much investment is speculative, and where both the risks and the possible social returns are great, it is appropriate that government invest in the future of young men and women who have much to offer and have received little.

### Obstacles to Youth Employment

No program of job or general economic development should be framed in a form or context which ignores the impact of the subeconomy. This will not be an easy task because many young men are cynical about the conventional programs and because the income produced through the subeconomy, though irregular and usually unpredictable, is immediate and sometimes substantial. Furthermore, there are powerful forces which have a stake in the subeconomy, or at least prefer to retain it as an alternative to more fundamental reform.

Certainly the potential advancement opportunity and income promised by job development programs, at the minimum, must match whatever tangible benefits are now derived from the sale of marijuana, pills, etc. This requirement is not observed by many of the manpower programs now on the books.

Perhaps more to the point is the question of what should be done about the subeconomy itself. One obvious alternative is to destroy it completely by a vigorous and uniform enforcement of law, an approach which (in the absence of the creation of other sources of income) could only lead to disaster. Without the economic support provided through this source, however risky and unreliable it may be, many youngsters and their families would be reduced to a condition of desperation and hopelessness. Furthermore, the cost of existing *limited* enforcement of laws against victimless crimes is already staggering, and a broader campaign could easily cause a breakdown in the entire law enforcement process. According to the *U.S. News and World Report* of October 26, 1970, more than $20 billion, of the total $51 billion in crime costs that year, were attributable to nonvictim crimes, such as narcotics, gambling, alcohol, prostitution, and abortion. According to another estimate, over one third of all law enforcement costs are related to nonvictim crimes. Efforts to enforce morality are not only abortive but unbearably costly.

A second alternative would be to legalize those offenses which do not involve injury to persons or property, and to treat such behavior as a health rather than a legal problem to the degree that it may have physical or emotional consequences. From a narrow economic viewpoint, it would seem logical to legalize the sale of marijuana under conditions similar to those now imposed on the sale of alcohol, and collect appropriate tax revenues from its distribution. A corollary proposal would involve the earmarking of revenues for exclusive use in community-improvement and job-creating projects run by indigenous nonprofit development corporations. With a requirement that a majority of the corporation's board of directors be drawn from a defined local area, there would then be an influential group of community residents who have an immediate stake in enforcement of the laws governing distribution of marijuana and prevention of its illegal manufacture.

While proposals of this nature will not easily or readily come to fruition, it should be quickly possible to deal with at least the more pressing aspects of those problems connected with unequal or excessively punitive law enforcement. Constitutional and legal rights relative to "search and seizure," requirements of "probable cause," and an adequate defense in criminal cases should be equally respected and enforced throughout the metropolitan area. Ex-offenders should have meaningful recourse to liberalized procedures for sealing and expungement of records. In this field, the Offender Rehabilitation Act should be passed by Congress, and the model statute drafted by Professor Miller and his associates at Georgetown should be implemented in all states. Both justice and common sense would seem to be served by an immediate provision that any arrest resulting from mistaken identity be automatically erased from the arrestee's record.[4]

These measures would give the ex-offender a second chance which in most cases he is denied. By combining them with far-reaching programs to validate existing job stipulations and remove discrimination against applicants with records unrelated to performance, government can offer the young men of Watts and east Los Angeles a realistic alternative to perpetual residence in the underworld of crime and the subeconomy. Under prevailing conditions, many of them have little option.

The opportunity for progress is at hand. The problems in Watts and east Los Angeles are formidable and complex, but hardly insoluble. The one essential precondition for their solution and for our collective survival is that we recognize the valuable resources already present in the community, and that we then act upon this knowledge.

NOTES

1. The tests offered at Oakland Community College in Rochester are designed "not only to measure such standard items as reading and mathematical ability, but also to evaluate decision-making and such abstract ideas as 'the sixth sense' (proprioceptivity), staged behavior (histrionics), physical coordination (kinesthetics), and knowledge of oneself." UPI dispatch, *Los Angeles Times*, December 5, 1971, p. 9. Another article in the *Times* (November 14, 1971, sec. H, p. 1) reports that a researcher in Princeton, New Jersey, estimates that about 80 per cent of those in the work force are now in the wrong jobs, in terms of their interests and real aptitudes.

2. *Newsweek* (August 30, 1971, pp. 74-75) has reported that Atlanta Area Technical School is a model post-secondary vocational training institution, with emphasis on producing instantly marketable skills.

3. Some Department of Human Resources Development offices in California already use radio stations and other media to communicate job information, a commendable innovation which should be vastly extended.

4. Police officers sometimes justify unnecessary detentions and/or arrests by claiming that they are searching for a suspect in a previous crime, or that the vehicle resembles one reported as stolen. There is reason to believe that these excuses are not always true. To deal with this problem, it might be useful to require every arresting officer to give the suspect his name, badge number, and the description of the real suspect or stolen vehicle as it is on file in the precinct station, should the arrestee request this information. The arrestee or his attorney would have the right to check those files quickly, and any failure to match descriptions on the part of the police would result in a quashing of the arrest.

# APPENDIX A

# Chart 1

## Comparative Statistics
### Los Angeles Low-Income Area Surveys

| | Area 1 CES White Spanish Males Ages 16-21 | Area 2 CES Negro Males Ages 16-21 | U.S. 1970 Negro Males Ages 16-21** | East Los Angeles IIR 16-24 | East Los Angeles IIR 16-19 | Watts IIR 16-24 | Watts IIR 16-19 |
|---|---|---|---|---|---|---|---|
| Total labor force | 4,552 | 6,919 | 724,000 | | | | |
| Unemployed (seeking work) | 996 | 2,575 | 164,000 | | | | |
| Regular unemployment rate | 21.9% | 37.2% | 22.6% | | | | |
| Discouraged workers* (lower) | 676 | 1,967 | 24,000*** | 0 | 0 | 0 | 0 |
| (higher) | 948 | 2,643 | | | | | |
| Adjusted unemployment rates* (lower) | 32.0% | 51.1% | | 30% | 34% | 46% | 62% |
| (higher) | 35.4% | 54.6% | | 67% | 65% | 52% | 38% |
| Labor force participation rate | 67.0% | 55.0% | 59.0% | 15.3% | | 35.5% | |
| Percent in families below poverty line (ages 16-24) | 15.9% | 23.7% | | | | | |
| Median family income (all households) | $7,736 | $6,439 | | | | | |

* Discouraged workers are defined as those who are now out of the labor force but either want a regular job immediately (the lower figure) or might want it (the higher figure). The adjusted unemployment rates are calculated by adding the discouraged workers to the regular unemployment and labor force figures. Unemployment figures in the IIR study include many of those elsewhere identified as "discouraged workers" (i.e., youngsters who are out of work and out of school and capable of working, but not currently seeking employment).

** Source: U.S. Bureau of Labor Statistics, Employment and Earnings, 1971.

*** Negro males 16-24 who think they cannot find a job.

NOTE: The Census Employment Survey (CES) was conducted in Los Angeles in August-December of 1970. Area 1 covers two low-income areas in the city which are predominantly Mexican-American in population. Area 2 covers three areas which are predominantly black.

## INSTITUTE OF LABOR AND INDUSTRIAL RELATIONS

All Americans have a vital stake in the shaping of sound public and private industrial relations policies and in the expansion of pertinent knowledge and skills. The Institute of Labor and Industrial Relations is a joint agency of The University of Michigan (Ann Arbor) and Wayne State University (Detroit). It was established in the spring of 1957 in order to maximize the contribution of each University, in activities related to industrial relations, to the people of Michigan and to the educational and research needs of workers and management.

The Institute has three major functions: first, to facilitate regular university instruction in the disciplines and professions related to industrial relations; second, to encourage basic and applied research on industrial relations topics; and third, to organize and promote programs of community education in industrial relations designed to serve labor, management and the public.

CHARLES M. REHMUS
*Co-Director*
The University of Michigan
Ann Arbor

RONALD W. HAUGHTON
*Co-Director*
Wayne State University
Detroit

*Policy Papers in Human Resources
and Industrial Relations*

LOUIS A. FERMAN, *Editor*

# ASPIRATION vs. OPPORTUNITY: "CAREERS" IN THE INNER CITY

POLICY PAPERS IN HUMAN RESOURCES
AND INDUSTRIAL RELATIONS 20

## Paul Bullock

INSTITUTE OF LABOR AND INDUSTRIAL RELATIONS
THE UNIVERSITY OF MICHIGAN—WAYNE STATE UNIVERSITY